tea

First published in the United States in 2006 by Chronicle Books LLC.
First published in France by Aubanel under the title *Le Thé, arômes & saveurs du monde*.

Copyright © 2005 by Aubanel, Paris.

Library of Congress Cataloging-in-Publication Data available.

ISBN-10 0-8118-5682-8
ISBN-13 978-0-8118-5682-9

Manufactured in China.

Distributed in Canada by Raincoast Books
9050 Shaughnessy Street
Vancouver, British Columbia V6P 6E5

10 9 8 7 6 5 4 3 2 1

Chronicle Books LLC
680 Second Street
San Francisco, California 94107

www.chroniclebooks.com

tea

Aromas and Flavors Around the World

by Lydia Gautier   *photographs by* Jean-François Mallet

CHRONICLE BOOKS

SAN FRANCISCO

FOREWORD

Tea is a drink that dates back across the centuries, forming part of the history of five continents, each country over time developing its own rituals and adapting the beverage to suit its own tastes. Good for the mind and good for the body, tea has always enjoyed an image of purity and serenity, but it is also a gourmet product with sensual qualities waiting to be discovered. During the last twenty years or so we have, in fact, witnessed not only a growing trend among Westerners to "rediscover" this drink, but also among the peoples of Asia, and among the Japanese in particular. Tea, with its regional roots and cultural associations, reflects both ancient and modern values, and is therefore an important aspect of the current lifestyle interest in food and world food.

My relationship with tea began some years ago once my palate had become educated to the taste of wine. I then discovered a richness and variety of aromatic qualities in tea comparable with those to be found in the great wine types. My studies as an agronomist specializing in tropical agriculture also played a part in my apprenticeship in the culture of tea, which I went on to pursue at the Palais des Thés in Paris for seven years, culminating in the opening of the École du Thé, a training center for the tasting and culture of tea.

But is another book on tea really necessary? Over the last ten years many books on this subject have appeared, from simple introductions to fine illustrated volumes. However, none has really addressed in depth the art of appreciating tea as one appreciates wine; none has really explored the evolution of its taste through the centuries. And yet tea – too often presented as a product of aesthetic, esoteric, and sterile qualities – has so much to offer in this respect.

The aim of this book is to explore tea in a detailed manner, in all its many aspects, and as a gastronomic product in its own right. The first chapter, A History of Tea, is devoted to the story of the dissemination of tea across the world; the development and great variety of tastes are explored through the practices and customs associated with the consumption of tea among different peoples and through the local recipes that punctuate this long journey and invite readers to explore and discover with their own palates.

In the following chapter, Alchemy of Tea, the agronomy and processing methods of the six different tea types – white, green, red, yellow, blue-green, and black – are examined in detail, highlighting their importance in revealing the aromatic bouquet of tea, as well as its benefits.

The next chapter, Tea Tasting, looks at this aspect from the point of view of enjoyment, technique (including other ways of preparing tea than the simple teapot used in the West), and professionalism (with tasting charts that can serve as useful reference tools for novice tea enthusiasts).

The Subtle Affinities of Tea is an opportunity to discover and explore interesting compatabilities with other worlds of taste – coffee, cocoa, wine – and also the sense of smell, through perfume.

Finally, the Address Book invites you to explore the tea merchants and tea rooms of the world. Enjoy your trip; enjoy your tea!

LYDIA GAUTIER

CONTENTS

I A HISTORY OF TEA

China, Japan, India, Great Britain, France, Morocco, the United States, Senegal, Mauritania, Afghanistan, Turkey ... In all these countries, tea is an everyday drink and, in some cases, has been for centuries. In others, though, it has only been drunk for a hundred years or so. A spiritual beverage associated with Buddhism in China, its country of origin, tea went on to conquer all the continents of the world, becoming a drink to be shared and given in hospitality. Whatever the country, whether consumer or producer, tea has been absorbed into its tradition and now forms part of the collective memory of the people as if it had always been there. Each country has also developed its own conventions for drinking tea and adapted it to suit the local palate, thus providing an opportunity for a wonderful journey of discovery for the senses across the continents.

CHINA, THE BIRTHPLACE OF TEA

THE ORIGINS OF TEA: A BITTER MEDICINAL PLANT

The tea plant, *Camellia sinensis*, originates in a region of the world extending from the golden triangle to the Yunnan mountains in China and the jungle of Assam in India.

The first written evidence dates back to around 200 years BCE (the Han period) and is found in a treatise on traditional Chinese medicine, the *Shen Nong Ben Cao Jin (Emperor Shen Nong's Treatise on Medicinal Plants*, written in honor of the legendary Shen Nong).

THE LEGEND OF HOW TEA WAS DISCOVERED
According to legend, tea was discovered by chance by Shen Nong, the father of agriculture and traditional medicine in China (also known as the "Divine Farmer") who reigned 2,737 years ago, when he was out cataloging plants that were of benefit to humankind and decided to take an afternoon rest. Shen Nong had an extraordinary physical feature: his stomach was transparent. This enabled him to observe how his organism reacted to different plants. Wishing to use his powers to the benefit of mankind, he advised people to boil water before drinking it in order to purify it. So, on this particular day, having dozed off under a tree, he awoke feeling thirsty. Some leaves from the tree fell into the water he was boiling, giving it a slight color. Curious, Shen Nong tasted this fortuitous beverage and found it to be very good, with a slight bitterness, and observing it in his stomach he saw that it was entirely beneficial. He had, of course, been sitting under a wild tea plant.

From earliest times, tea has been recognized for its purifying and fortifying qualities. It also clears the mind. The Chinese ideogram for tea bears witness to the fact that it is good for human beings.

Before becoming known as *cha* in the eighth century, in ancient times it had been called *tu* ("bitter, edible plant") or *ming*, which means "buds," the Chinese having noticed that the buds were the best part of the plant.

LU YU (733–804), THE FIRST TEA MASTER, SWEETENED THE BITTER TEA PLANT

The birth of the art of tea

The art of tea – that is to say, the art of producing and tasting tea – emerged during the eighth century under the Tang dynasty (618–907). It was the subject of a work written by Lu Yu, *Le Classique du thé* (*The Classic of Tea*), which remains a source of reference today. Lu Yu describes the early principles of the production, processing, and tasting of tea. Born in the province of Hubei, Lu Yu was a Buddhist monk who combined his spiritual quest with the study of tea. He lived as a hermit in Nanjing in Jiangsu province, known for its tea, and devoted his life to the art of tea.

Green tea soup

Lu Yu explained how to sweeten the bitterness of tea. He stressed the importance of harvesting in spring, as this produced the tastiest buds. Once the buds were picked, he recommended several stages of processing – steaming, rolling, grinding, drying, tying, packaging – to produce a cake of dried tea known as a "tea moon." The process Lu Yu described suggests that the tea cakes in question were made of green tea. A "tea moon" of this kind weighed approximately 8 ounces (250 grams), making it easy to transport and preserve.

Tea was prepared as a decoction, and Lu Yu recommended adding no more than a pinch of salt to heighten the aromas. This was known as a "soup," as the leaves were also eaten. The ritual of preparing and consuming tea was very important and directly associated with the art of living.

PRECEDING DOUBLE PAGE:
Old nomad woman drinking tea in the Pir Panjal mountains, Jammu-Kashmir, India.

Labookellie tea plantation, Sri Lanka.

ABOVE, FROM LEFT TO RIGHT:
Modern compressed tea cake from Yunnan province, similar to Lu Yu's "tea moon."

The Chinese symbol for tea, cha (pronounced tcha): it consists of three keys which are, from top to bottom, that of herb, human, and tree; it can therefore be translated as a herb that grows on a tree and is good for humans.

[1] *From* Le Classique du
thé (The Classic of Tea),
*by Lu Yu, translated by
Sister Jean-Marie Vianney,
published by Morel, 1977.*

Boiled tea, "the sweet dew and the fine flower of cream"

Lu Yu stressed the importance of the bitter-sweet quality of the taste of tea. Bitterness is a characteristic of the plant, while sweetness is introduced by the way the leaves are treated during processing. According to Lu Yu, a good tea should be "bitter in the mouth and sweet in the throat." He compared the aromas of tea with "sweet dew," evoking its purity and power to refresh, and with "the fine flower of cream" (clarified butter) in terms of its smoothness. He wrote: "When tea has a delicate perfume, it is called *chia*. If it is less fragrant and has a bitter, strong taste, it is called *ch'uan*. If it is bitter or strong in the mouth but sweet when swallowed, it is called *ch'a*."[1]

The drink of Buddhism

Following in the tradition of Lu Yu, the *chan* Buddhist monks (who gave Zen to Japan) played their part in the development of tea cultivation by planting tea bushes around their monasteries – as they would drink tea during meditation sessions. The peasants, who lived under a feudal system, paid tribute to the

emperor in the form of the finest harvest of all: the buds alone. This premium harvest is still known as the imperial harvest. At the same time, the nomadic peoples of western China, the Mongols, Tartars, Turks, and Tibetans, who themselves boasted a rare commodity – horses – which they could exchange for tea, made this drink an integral part of their daily life. The Tang dynasty even created an Office of Tea and Horses (the *Cha Ma Si*) to manage this important trade; this organization continued to operate until the fall of the empire in 1911. These peoples enhanced the tea soup with citrus peel, with fruits such as jujube and dogwood berries, and with spices, onion, aromatic herbs, and cereal flour.

Tea with butter and salt, the ancestral drink of the ethnic peoples of the mountains and steppes

The Mongols, Tibetans, Nepalese, and certain other ethnic groups from the mountains of Yunnan still drink tea prepared as a decoction, churned with rancid butter and salt. These different groups discovered that the addition of tea leaves to their soup helped to compensate for numerous deficiencies in their diet, which

*Old Chinese tea kettle
steaming at Mademoiselle
Li's tea salon in Paris.*

is low in fresh fruit and vegetables. The tea used is compressed tea, coming mainly from Yunnan and Sichuan, and also from a small local production source in Tibet.

Below is a recipe for this winter beverage using ingredients that are easy to find.

TEA WITH SALTED BUTTER

2 PINTS/1 LITER OF WATER
1 PINT/1/2 LITER OF WHOLE MILK
2 OUNCES/50 GRAMS OF SEMI-SALTED BUTTER
1 OUNCE/30 GRAMS OF BRICK TEA

Boil the water with the tea for a few minutes; add the milk and leave to simmer for 3 to 4 minutes. Remove from the heat and add the semi-salted butter, stirring vigorously to produce a smoothly blended mixture. Pour through a strainer and serve in bowls.

EMPEROR HUIZHONG (1082–1135) REFINED TEA DRINKING

Letters of nobility

Emperor Huizhong of the Song dynasty (960–1279) – also known as the "crowned dreamer," as he was versed in the arts and politics – introduced tea to the royal court by writing the *Da Guan Cha Lun* (*Discussions on Tea during the Da Guan Era*). Tea was therefore no longer drunk exclusively by Buddhists but became the empire's most important beverage, the emperor himself taking the title of tea master.

Whisked green tea

Huizhong recommended grinding the tea broken off from the green "tea moon" into a very fine powder by putting it through a small grinder. The tea powder was then blended with warm water by whisking it in the bowl itself with a small whisk. This new method of preparation brought further refinement to the art of tea practiced in a spirit of celebration and communion. The process from preparation to tasting gave rise to an entire ritual with the use of fine objects to show the tea to best advantage. It was an art that took root in Japan at this period.

"Aromatic, sweet, and delicate" tea

At that time, the term bitter had a negative connotation. Aromatic persistency was the preferred term. In the *Da Guan Cha Lun*, Huizhong writes about a highly regarded tea from the province of Fujian: "Taste. The most important aspect of tea is taste. The ideal taste consists of aromatics, sweetness, and delicacy. Only Heyuan tea produced in Beiyuan encompasses all these qualities. If the taste is pure but lacks character, this means that it has been exposed and crushed for too long."[2]

THE MING DYNASTY (1368–1644) POPULARIZED AND EXPORTED TEA DRINKING

From tea to teas: the explosion of tea colors

The first Ming emperor, who was the son of a peasant, reorganized the world of agriculture by breaking up the great feudal estates into small, independent farms. He encouraged the expansion of tea cultivation and, to make it more profitable, ordered the production process to be simplified by eliminating the final milling stage, which was costly in terms of both energy and time. This gave rise to the loose tea with which we are familiar in the West. Tea then set out to conquer new markets: tea consumption became widespread among the different social groups in China and won over western drinkers as early as the fourteenth century. To meet the ever-growing demand, small producers diversified their product range: this led to the explosion of different tea colors, which then began to be drunk in the way that is still familiar to us today, with the majority of Chinese preferring to drink green tea.

The main tea-producing provinces – Zhejiang, Jiangsu, Anhui, Fujian, Guangdong, Hunan, Sichuan, Yunnan, and Hubei – all situated in the southern half of China, were the same as they are today. Tea production in Taiwan also dates from this period. The island was annexed by the Chinese at the end of the seventeenth century, and it was the new arrivals from the Chinese province of Fujian who introduced tea plants to the island, which was extremely fertile and provided ideal growing conditions. They are known in particular for diversifying the production methods of blue-green teas (known as *wu long* or *Oolong*), and became masters of the art of producing and tasting these teas.

THE SEVENTEENTH CENTURY: THE INTRODUCTION OF SMOKED TEA — A TEA FOR EXPORT

This is one of many stories associated with the creation of this type of tea. A tea producer in Fujian province had sold a European merchant a large shipment of green tea. The merchant had, of course, paid for it all in advance. Just before it was due to be shipped, the producer suffered a flood at his warehouse and, in order to deliver the tea on time, dried the leaves over a wood fire, where the leaves absorbed the smell of the smoke.

OPPOSITE:
Large Yixing teapot at Mademoiselle Li's tea salon in Paris. Yixing teapots originally had a capacity of about 2 pints (1 liter). They were made smaller over the years to give better concentration and improve the aroma of the tea.

ABOVE:
Tea picking in China, nineteenth-century engraving.

[2] *From* Asie: savourer, goûter (Asia: Savor, Taste)*, volume III, article by Marco Ceresa, editor Flora Blanchon, PUF, 1995.*

ABOVE:
A legacy of the Ming dynasty that conquered the salons of Europe: blue-and-white porcelain.

OPPOSITE:
Yixing earthenware teapot engraved with the verse: "A good tea leaves a sweet aftertaste in the throat, and it is this that gives great pleasure," Thés de Chine, Paris.

The close connection between the master potters and the world of scholars played an important part in the fame of Yixing ware; the teapots were inscribed by great poets, which enhanced their value.

He remained quiet about the incident when he shipped the tea out, and expected to receive no further orders from the merchant. However, the following year the merchant ordered twice the amount! Smoked tea, often known in the West as China tea, is therefore a tea produced solely for export, and has never been drunk by the Chinese.

Traditionally, teas that are lightly smoked are called *Lapsang Souchong* and the more heavily smoked teas are known as *Tarry Souchong*.

"Sweet and mellow" tea

Many books on the art of preparing and enjoying tea were written by specialists during this period. Around 1570, Lu Shusheng, a tea master, gave some advice in his *Tea House Report* (*Chaliao ji*): "Tea tasting. Take a mouthful of tea. First swill it around your mouth, then swallow it slowly and wait for a gentle salivation to immerse your tongue. This is how one attains the true nature of tea. If one mixes it with other products, one takes away its taste."[3] Around 1604, another tea master, Chang Yongbing, records in his *Register of Tea* (*Chalu*) the characteristics of good and bad tea: "Assess the essential qualities. Does the tea have any essential characteristics? Yes. Aroma, color, and taste are the constituent characteristics of tea … The best tastes are those that are sweet and mellow. Tastes that are smooth and light are ordinary. Tastes that are bitter and astringent are inferior to these."[4]

Gastronomy and everyday consumption

The appearance of the teapot

Ceramicists expanded the range of utensils used to enhance the subtle aromas of each different tea color. The method of preparation was simplified: the leaves were now infused whole but no longer eaten. Loose tea needed a vessel in which to be steeped, so the teapot was created. The most ancient teapots found at Chinese archaeological sites date back to the early sixteenth century.

Yixing clay teapots are one of the hallmarks of the Ming dynasty. Yixing is a small town in the Chinese province of Jiangsu, 186 miles (300 kilometers) west of Shanghai. The surrounding area is rich in deposits of purple

PRECEDING DOUBLE PAGE :
The tea house, a meeting place where you can drink tea, eat dim sum (baskets of steamed dumplings), and display your birds, Wan Loy tea house, Hong Kong, 1980.

ABOVE :
Gaiwan (*or zhong*): *a lidded bowl with saucer, used traditionally in China for drinking green tea, Thés de Chine, Paris.*

OPPOSITE :
Traditional interior of a Chinese tea house in the heart of Paris, Mademoiselle Li's tea salon at the Jardin d'Acclimatation.

[3] *From* Asie: savourer, goûter, *volume III, op. cit.*

[4] *From* Asie: savourer, goûter, *volume III, op. cit.*

[5] *From* Asie: savourer, goûter, *volume III, op. cit.*

clay, the grain of which is so fine that after firing it becomes almost as delicate as porcelain. Yixing pots became the standard for preparing semi-oxidized teas in the gong fu cha method, as the fine, uniform quality of the pores allows optimum oxygenation of the tea infusion. Naturally, the beauty of Yixing ware also resides in the artistic skill of the master potter, and in its "memory" of successive infusions. There is a veritable art involved in the "seasoning" of the teapot. This is entrusted to a tea master who sometimes takes several years to season it to perfection.

Repeated infusions

As tea leaves were no longer eaten, they could be used again to make fresh infusions. In 1597, Xu Ciyu in his *Commentary on Tea* (*Chasu*) advised only two changes of water using the same leaves: "Tasting. Tea in a teapot may be used twice only; the first time it is flavorful, the second it is sweet and pure … If one leaves it for a short time and allows the temperature to drop, a tea that is strong and bitter (negative qualities) may be obtained."[5]

Tasting tools

a) *The* gong fu cha *method*

The art of *gong fu cha*, or the mastery of time and action in the preparation of tea, came into being with the creation of Yixing ware. Taoist in inspiration, this method of preparation is a sensual and hedonistic way of enjoying tea. It ensures that the aromatic complexity of

Oolong and black teas – which are prepared in strong concentrations and infused several times – are fully appreciated. The equipment used is deliberately small in scale, the key element usually being the small Yixing-ware teapot.

b) The gaiwan *(or* zhong) *method*

The *gaiwan*, a porcelain bowl with a saucer and lid, also appeared under the Ming dynasty and is still used daily in tea houses. It is an excellent tasting implement both for infusing and revealing the subtle aromas of green, white, and yellow teas.

Tea houses

The tea house became an important feature of social life in China. People came to tea houses to discuss and settle matters – from business negotiations to disputes requiring mediation. Bird enthusiasts came to take a rest after showing off their blackbirds and canaries. Additionally, people spent the day there playing mah-jong. As well as tea, you could drink sake, and sample cakes and simple dishes such as noodles with meat. These tea houses, which were very popular under the Ming dynasty and became a symbol of the empire, disappeared under the Cultural Revolution. They are now beginning to reappear to some extent in the cities of mainland China. In Taiwan a new type of tea house began to appear in the late 1970s: the *chayiguan* (tea art house), where one can sample the great classic teas.

Modern times: everyday teas and luxury teas

It was under the Ming dynasty that tea began to be drunk in the way it still is today. It is now a veritable living art with differently formed teas appearing each year, improvements in the production process, and the active pursuit of maximum aromatic quality combined with color. Research institutes now work on production sites to ensure ongoing innovation. Tea has become a plant of great artistic and commercial value, and the subject of much research and speculation. This is also true of other arts associated with tea – ceramics in particular.

Tea remains a popular everyday beverage, consumed on the streets, like water. This tea is generally a medium-quality green tea. At the same time, with the economic development of China and the increased standard of living, growing numbers of stylish tea-art houses serving the great classic teas are now opening and enjoying great success. The tea served and sold in such outlets is considered to be a luxury, gourmet product.

[6] *From* La Maison de thé (The Tea House), *by Lao She, translated by Chaguan, published by Langues étrangères, 1980.*

I, Yang the imbecile, with my bamboo sticks, arrive at the tea house.
The Yutai house, forty years old,
Enjoys a flourishing trade.
The atmosphere animated, the clients numerous …
Young and old, bird, cricket, grasshopper enthusiasts
Drink quality tea here,
And enjoy good food.
Solely those who have no money
Can eat with their eyes only!
One can play chess
Placing bets with peppered balls!
Over there some important gentlemen,
Turn a coughing fit into an event!
But above all, beware of one thing –
Never mention the government! [6]

FROM *LA MAISON DE THÉ (THE TEA HOUSE)*, BY LAO SHE (1899–1966): A PLAY SET IN A TEA HOUSE IN PEKING; THE FIRST ACT TAKES PLACE IN 1896.

The traditional gaiwan, *an everyday object in China, Chengdu, China, 1995.*

OPPOSITE:

Tea utensils at Mademoiselle Li's tea salon in Paris.

GREEN TEA CROSSES THE SEA OF JAPAN

TEA, SAMURAI, AND ZEN: THE STORY OF A BITTER, SMOOTH JADE-GREEN POWDER

TEA AND BUDDHISM: THE LEGEND OF BODDHI DHARMA

According to one Japanese legend, this is how tea drinking was invented. The Indian prince Boddhi Dharma left his kingdom to devote his life to Buddhism and decided to embark on a pilgrimage that would last several years, vowing never to sleep. After leaving India he began to travel through China to reach the land of the rising sun. On the way he fell asleep and, according to certain versions, fell prey to erotic dreams. On awaking, in his fury he cut off his eyelids and buried them at the side of the road. Some time later, when he was traveling back down the road, he found that a bush had sprung up there with leaves shaped like eyelids. Filled with wonder, he picked some shoots and ate them; this helped him to meditate for many hours at a time without falling asleep, and the custom of drinking tea was born.

From imported tea to indigenous tea

Introduced by Buddhist monks, tea was drunk in Japan from the ninth century. It was imported from China in the form of tea cakes and consumed in the Lu Yu style. It was during the twelfth century that Eisai the monk (1141–1215) began importing the seeds of the tea plant and started tea cultivation in the Japanese archipelago, first on the island of Kyushu, then on Honshu, and most importantly at Uji near Kyoto. At that time, it was prepared in the same way as in China, and all the equipment used was imported from China.

From the world of the monastery to that of the shogun

Gradually, the shogun world succumbed to the delights of tea, and by the thirteenth century it had become central to the life of the samurai soldier. The samurai appointed their own tea master, a Zen Buddhist monk, who prepared them for combat by performing the tea ceremony to purify them and give them strength. The tea master played an important part in political decision-making, at times

Tea plantation in Shizuoka district, with snow-capped Mount Fuji in the background, Japan.

becoming the samurai's confidant. Until the fifteenth century, the tea ceremony was synonymous with ostentation. Competitions were organized in palace rooms to show off the finest Chinese accessories, local Japanese equipment being denigrated.

The birth of a dissident movement: austerity and sobriety

In the late fifteenth century, the tea masters began to aspire to a less sophisticated form of ceremony, one closer to its monastic Zen origins. The ceremonial rooms were abandoned in favor of what became known as a tea pavilion, the *soan* ("house of the poor" or "cottage"), which was hidden away in a garden. Powdered green tea, *maccha*, was prepared using rustic tools. The only decoration in the *soan* was a vase of flowers and a scroll with Zen calligraphy or a drawing. This new style of tea drinking reached its peak with Takeno Jōō (1502–1555), who developed the *wabi* concept in relation to tea.

This concept, which literally means "frozen, withered beauty," attributes beauty and worth to items that are imperfect, incomplete, or irregular. Sen Rikyū (1522–1591), his disciple,

laid down the foundations, still in force today, of *cha do* ("the way of tea") or *cha no yu* ("hot water in tea"), which is based on four principles – harmony (*wa*); respect (*kei*); purity (*sei*); and the synthesis of these three qualities, serenity (*jaku*) – and on the seven rules reproduced below.

Make a delicious bowl of tea.
Set down some charcoal to heat the water.
Arrange some flowers as they are found in the fields.
In summer, evoke coolness; in winter, heat.
Anticipate the weather in each thing.
Prepare yourself for rain.
Show every possible consideration for your guests.[7]

[7] *From* Vie du thé, esprit du thé (Tea Life, Tea Mind) *by Soshitsu Sen, published by Jean Cyrille Godefroy, 1994.*

OPPOSITE:
Interior of a tea room in a tea pavilion in Kyoto.

ABOVE, FROM TOP TO BOTTOM:

The stages of the cha no yu *tea ceremony at the Chajin Japanese tea salon in the center of Paris.*

1. The mistress of the ceremony conducts a symbolic purification with the fukusa, *a small square of silk.*

2. She draws water with a large bamboo ladle, the hishaku, *and pours it into a cast-iron kettle over heat; on the left of the fire is the cold-water pot, the* mizusashi, *used to adjust the temperature of the water.*

3. She prepares the bowl of tea by whisking maccha *powder with a small bamboo whisk, the* chasen,

having taken a little maccha *powder from the red box, the* natsume, *using a bamboo scoop, the* chashaku.

4. She offers the bowl of tea to the guest who handles it with great delicacy and respect; in the background is the tokonoma, *a small alcove with a* kakemono *and a flower, the* chabana; *the* chabana *must be fresh, simple, and unscented, embodying nature in its purity; the* kakemono *may be either a scroll painting or inscribed with calligraphy for a more formal ceremony. These two objects present the atmosphere in which the mistress of the ceremony wishes the guest to be immersed.*

BELOW:
Shelf of chawan, *Japanese ceremonial bowls, by contemporary Japanese artists, Chajin tea salon, Paris. The bowl on the top left is in the traditional Raku shape.*

OPPOSITE:
Detail from a Japanese print of the tea ceremony, Nara, Japan.

FOLLOWING DOUBLE PAGE:
Cha no yu *ceremony at Chajin tea salon, Paris.*

Tea objects

Sen Rikyū commissioned local craftsmen to make tea objects, in particular the *chawan* ("tea bowl"), the central element of the tea ceremony, and abandoned the use of ceramics imported from China. He discovered a potter called Chojiro, who made bowls that fitted in perfectly with the *wabi* philosophy, and ennobled him. Until then potters had not been entitled to bear a family name. Chojiro received the name *Raku*, which means "joy." Today, the fifteenth *Raku*, Kichizaemon XV, born in 1948, continues to create ceramics for Japanese tea masters. Sen Rikyū also developed the concept of *soan*, using local, rustic materials in the construction of tea pavilions, such as clay and straw for the walls, bamboo for the windows, Japanese cedar for the beams, and thatch for the roof. This revolutionized Japanese architecture, which until that time had been inspired by Chinese architecture, and laid the foundations of contemporary Japanese architecture.

The stages of the tea ceremony

The *cha no yu* ("hot water in the tea") ceremony extends over an entire day, punctuated by periods in the garden, a light meal (*kaiseki*), the serving of strong tea (*koicha*), and then light tea (*usucha*).

Everything, from the accessories used in preparing the tea to the way the tea room is arranged, is planned in accordance with the event being celebrated. At the entrance to the tea room an alcove, the *tokonoma*, contains a floral decoration, the *chabana* (an arrangement consisting of a single flower, distinct from the *ikebana*, which contains several flowers) and some calligraphy, which together set the tone for the atmosphere that the master of the ceremony wishes to create. The guests bow in front of the *tokonoma* and the hearth, where the kettle is placed as a sign of respect, and then sit down on the tatamis. The master of the ceremony brings the equipment needed to prepare the tea and purifies it symbolically with the *fukusa*, a small square of silk. He serves the cake that is eaten before drinking the tea to coat the palate in sugar and to prepare it for the bitterness and smoothness of the whisked tea. He then prepares the *maccha* (*koicha* or *usucha*), which has been blended into hot water, and serves it. When drinking strong tea, which is only lightly mixed producing a very dense foamless emulsion, the cake (*omogashi*) is fresh and creamy. When drinking light tea, which is aerated and foamy, the cake (*higashi*) is dry and very sugary. The aim of the ceremony is to enter into communion with oneself and with the other persons present.

MACCHA CAKE

A recipe devised by Tea Master Kazuyo Ishii-Coineau of the Chajin tea salon in Paris. *(The* maccha *used for the recipe in the photograph is* Maccha Ryori *from Chajin.)*

SERVES 6

³/₄ OUNCE/20 GRAMS OF MACCHA

5 OUNCES/140 GRAMS OF SUPERFINE SUGAR

2 GOOD TEASPOONS OF SENCHA TEA

3¹/₂ OUNCES/100 GRAMS OF BUTTER
(AT ROOM TEMPERATURE)

3 MEDIUM EGGS

3 OUNCES/80 GRAMS OF WHEAT FLOUR

1¹/₂ OUNCES/40 GRAMS OF CHESTNUT FLOUR

1 TEASPOON OF BAKING POWDER

1 PINCH OF SALT

Preheat the oven to 410°F/210°C. Sieve the maccha; *mix it with the sugar. Infuse the* sencha *tea in a small 10-fluid-ounce/30-centiliter teapot; once tepid, pour over the sweetened* maccha; *mix together to obtain a thickish mixture, which is not too runny. Add the butter and the beaten eggs. Mix together the two types of flour and the baking powder, and combine them with the mixture, folding them in with a spatula. Add the salt. Pour the mixture into a 10-inch/25-cm cake pan lined with waxed paper. Place in the oven and cook for 1 hour at 300°F/150°C. Cover with aluminum foil toward the end of cooking so that the cake retains its attractive green color.*

THE TEA OF SCHOLARS: A FRESH, PLANT LIQUOR

The second method of drinking tea, currently the most widespread in Japan as it is the most accessible (requiring a simpler form of preparation), is a legacy of the Ming period. Again, it was a monk who introduced this new method of production and consumption, at the beginning of the Edo era (1603–1867), a period of pacification and blossoming of the arts. The art of tea became widely practiced in intellectual circles inspired by the *furyu* ("wind flow") philosophy, advocating a taste for simplicity and natural beauty. The *sencha do* ceremony, far more hedonistic than the *cha do* – in fact, similar to the Chinese *gong fu cha* – was mainly practiced in spring to celebrate the rebirth of nature and the arrival of the finest classic teas, including *gyokuro*, one of Japan's most highly prized teas. The tea is infused in small teapots and served in small bowls. On this occasion, the cake is eaten after the first infusion. The bulk of the production (80 percent) is concentrated in the Shizuoka district, near Tokyo.

TEA: A TRADITIONAL AND CONTEMPORARY LIVING ART

An everyday drink, a luxurious ceremonial drink

The Japanese still drink a large quantity of very hot green tea with their meals. These are medium-quality teas, often roasted, such as the roast green tea Bancha Hojicha. They also drink many green teas and Oolong teas – the latter being imported from Taiwan – iced and unsweetened, and sold in small bottles. However, this does not stop them spending a fortune on fine spring-harvested teas consumed on their own, so that they can be properly appreciated. Tea ceremonies are conducted by Zen monks in their monasteries at certain periods of the year and taught in tea schools. Such ceremonies require a room arranged in a certain way and a great deal of equipment, and are therefore rarely practiced at home.

O cha and *ko cha*, or how the West seduced Japan

Just as Japanese tea and its ceremonial aspects found an appreciative audience in the West, "Western-style" tea – that is to say, oxidized and aromatized tea – appealed to the Japanese. This was a genuine cultural exchange in which tea drinking became synonymous with travel and luxury. In fact, alongside the tea they drank every day, it became very fashionable for the Japanese to go to English-style tea rooms and drink Indian, Sri Lankan, and perfumed teas (such as apple, strawberry, and vanilla). French brands in particular are highly prized, a byword for luxury, and Japanese tourists return home from their travels with packets of tea as gifts. The Japanese also have different names to distinguish between foreign tea and their own: *o cha* is Japanese tea, and *ko cha* ("small tea") is Western-style tea.

The virtues of tea

Historically, in Japan, tea has always been associated with well-being. Japanese laboratories were in fact the first to undertake serious research into the properties of tea. As Japan produced only green tea, this was the only type that they analyzed. Consequently, the first results on the beneficial qualities of tea related only to green tea. In Japan, green tea has been used for many years in cosmetics due to its antioxidant properties. And since the 1990s, tea producers in the Shizuoka region have even been publishing cookbooks with recipes based on green tea, in response to a growing desire to eat more healthily. Many foods and edible goods using *maccha* are now available – for example, chewing gum, ice cream, sweets, pastries, and soups.

AMA CHA OR BUDDHA TEA

In Japan, a plant infusion known as *ama cha* (which literally means "sweet tea") is traditionally drunk on April 8 each year to celebrate the first bath of the infant Buddha (the *Kanbutsu-e*). This corresponds to a festival known as the Flower Festival (*Hana Matsuri*), as it is the time of year when the cherry trees come into blossom. This plant, which has nothing to do with *Camellia sinensis*, is a creeper of the hydrangea family: *Hydrangea serrata*. Its leaves, when harvested and laid out to dry, oxidize naturally and take on a green-brown color. The liquor they produce is very sweet with a marked sugary flavor and licorice aromas.

ABOVE:
As well as its traditional use in tea ceremonies, maccha *is often used in cooking in Japan. After working with French master confectioners, the Japanese pastry chef Sadaharu Aoki combined the tradition of* maccha *in cooking with Western recipes. Above left are white chocolate truffles flavored with maccha, Sadaharu Aoki, Paris.*

A traditional tea merchant's selling great classic teas, Ippôdo, Kyoto, Japan.

FOLLOWING DOUBLE PAGE:
Jade-green maccha *powder.*

CARAVANS OF TEA BRICKS HEAD OUT TO CENTRAL ASIA AND THE MIDDLE AND NEAR EAST

SPICE ROUTES, TEA ROUTES

Many commodities such as spices and silk were transported on camel and horseback from ancient times. The routes they followed started in central China, crossed the Gobi Desert, and headed to the Pamir region, and the city of Kashgar in particular, which was the principal trading post for caravan traders from east and west. The caravans continued their journey crossing northern Afghanistan and then skirting the Caspian Sea to the north or south to reach the Mediterranean. It was via this land route that the Arabs in the ninth century discovered tea, as one of these routes crossed the Arabian peninsula.

OPPOSITE, FROM LEFT TO RIGHT:
Father and child drinking tea in a nomad encampment, Jammu–Kashmir, India.

Monpa child warming himself with a cup of tea, Arunāchal Pradesh, India.

Chinese green tea shaped like flowers on sale in a tea store in Moscow, Russia.

The emperor has a monopoly on salt and on the plant known as sakh [tea] from which the Chinese make an infusion with hot water and which is sold in every town for considerable sums of money. This plant has more leaves than clover, is more perfumed, but is bitter. They boil water and pour it on to the plant. The Chinese use it for everything.

ACCOUNT BY AN UNNAMED ARAB, NINTH CENTURY

The peoples of central Asia and the Middle and Near East also discovered tea as a result of these trading caravans. However, the transportation of tea via caravan appears to have come to a halt in Libya. Tea did not cross the Sahara and did not travel much further west: there is no written evidence of tea being consumed in these areas prior to the eighteenth century.

THE CONCENTRATED AND FULL-BODIED TASTE OF TEA PREPARED IN A SAMOVAR

In that part of the world that stretches from central Asia to Arabia in the southwest and to Russia in the north, tea has been drunk for centuries throughout the day, in a very concentrated form – sometimes even boiled. This tea is the red tea that is obtained from a blend of classic teas of different origins, historically Chinese, and currently Indian, Sri Lankan, Kenyan, and Turkish, producing a full-bodied, copper-colored liquor. In some countries such as Turkey, Iran, Afghanistan, and Russia, a special piece of equipment is used – the samovar, which provides a constant source of hot water. The name comes from the Russian *samo* (oneself) and *var* (to boil). Mongolian in origin, this large vessel has a central chimney that is filled with hot embers to keep the water heated. The teapot is placed above it, filled with very concentrated tea, prepared from a large dose of tea leaves heavily steeped at the start of the day. Tea can be served from it all day long by pouring concentrated tea into a cup and diluting it with hot water from the samovar to suit one's taste.

Before drinking this piping-hot beverage, a lump of sugar or a spoonful of jam is allowed to dissolve on the tongue to prepare the palate for the astringency and bitterness of the tea. Sometimes spices such as cardamom and saffron are added.

SAMOVAR TEA: HOT TEA AVAILABLE ALL DAY LONG

The principle is simple: a small teapot of concentrated tea and plenty of hot water with which to dilute it.

If you do not have a samovar, you can use a thermos filled with boiling water. At the start of the day, make a strong infusion of red tea (Chinese Keemun or Yunnan tea, Ceylon or Assam) or black tea (basic Pu Er). To do this, use double the normal amount of tea (approximately 3/4 ounce/20 grams to 1 pint/1/2 liter) and steep for 5 minutes regardless of the type of tea. The teas suggested are relatively stable, that is to say, their flavor will change little as they cool, the concentrated liquor oxidizing very slowly, unlike red teas such as Darjeeling or other colors of tea.

ABOVE:
Nineteenth-century
Russian brass samovar,
Kusmi Tea, Paris.

OPPOSITE:
Elderly Lebanese man
making tea in his store,
Baalbek.

There is no need to use grand cru teas: middle-of-the-range, full-bodied, aromatic teas, whether broken- or whole-leaf, are perfectly adequate. Once the tea has steeped, strain and store it in a small, 1 pint/¹/₂-liter teapot. Pour a little of the concentrated tea into a cup and dilute with water from the thermos, as desired, throughout the day. Sugar, milk, jam, spices, or citrus peel may be added if wished. Spices and citrus peel may also be added to the tea while it is infusing.

RUSSIA: THE WORLD'S LARGEST TEA IMPORTER

The Russian Federation: a major tea consumer

The Russian Federation is currently the world's largest tea importer. High-altitude, quality tea is also produced near Krasnodar and on the shores of the Black Sea on the border with Georgia, close to Sochi and Adler. However, this production accounts for less than 1 percent of national consumption: in 1999, 177,500 short tons (161,000 metric

tons) of tea were imported, compared with the 14,300 short tons (13,000 metric tons) produced. In Russia tea is drunk by over 80 percent of the population on a daily basis; it is the least costly drink available, even cheaper than milk. It was classified as a basic commodity in the "shopping basket" used to calculate minimum subsistence levels. Tea is therefore on the list of food products whose supply to remote areas is the responsibility of the federal and government authorities. The first really lasting contact appears to be relatively recent in terms of tea caravans, dating only from the seventeenth century. Tea was among the gifts sent by the emperor of China to the czars, who were captivated by this beneficial plant. Around 1689, Peter the Great set up a special trading caravan to exchange furs for chests of tea. Some 300 camels wended their way across 9,321 miles (15,000 kilometers) taking over a year and providing a link between Moscow and China.

As in other tea-drinking countries, in Russia tea was originally a drink reserved for the elite but consumption gradually became more widespread. Indeed, after a few centuries it had become an everyday drink consumed by Russians in both town and country, and at all social levels – aristocratic, bourgeois, and

ABOVE, FROM LEFT TO RIGHT:
Shoe merchant and tanner sipping glasses of tea on the street, Baalbek, Lebanon.

Display of tea glasses at the Pierre Loti café in Istanbul, Turkey.

Collection of Russian tea caddies from different periods, Kusmi Tea, Paris.

working class. It even entered popular language: the word for "tip" is *na chai*, which literally means "for tea." Tea is consumed at home, on the street, in establishments similar to Chinese tea houses, known as *chai-naya*; it evens forms part of the 24-ruble "trans-Siberian pack," which contains the basics required for sleeping and for making a cup of tea.

The taste of tea

In those days the teas consumed were therefore compressed green or red Chinese teas, and continued to be so until recent times. Nowadays the majority of the tea drunk in Russia is Indian (over 70 percent of imported tea) and Sri Lankan (16 percent of imported tea): it is therefore mainly red tea with a slight increase in green tea that enjoys a good reputation as being "healthy."

The origin of "Goût Russe" teas

Tea merchants refer to certain blends of tea of different origins as "Goût Russe" teas: some are perfumed, some not, some are flavored with citrus-peel essential oils and sometimes with spices. In the case of unperfumed "Goût Russe" teas, Russians traditionally blended classic teas of various origins to produce a taste they liked, generally full-bodied and powerful, sometimes with a slightly smoky note. However, in the case of perfumed "Goût Russe" teas, historically it was the caravans that introduced the custom of tea boiled with citrus peel that originated under the Tang dynasty, although there are no written records of this type of tea being drunk among Russian society. On the other hand, the habit of drinking such teas was introduced in the West during the 1950s by a French importer, Jean Jumeau-Lafond. In response to British Earl Grey, he created the first blend based on red tea and citrus, which he called *Goût Russe Douchka* in honor of his Russian wife who liked to squeeze quarter of an orange into her cup of hot tea.

ABOVE, FROM LEFT TO RIGHT:
Turkish tea served in a small, transparent, tulip-shaped glass known as a bardak, *Grand Bazaar, Istanbul, Turkey.*

Kusmi Tea, a traditional Russian tea blend. Founded in 1867 in St. Petersburg by Pavel Michailovitch Kousmichoff, the Kousmichoff ("Kusmi") tea house, was the purveyor of tea to the court of the czars. Just before the 1917 revolution, the Kusmi tea house had more than 50 stores in Russia and a branch in London at 11 Queen Victoria Street. However, sensing danger, Viatcheslav Kousmichoff, head of the company, transferred the family business to Paris, to 75 Avenue Niel, where it continues trading today.

The podstakannik, *the traditional Russian tea glass with a metal handle and support; the use of this glass dates back to the early twentieth century.*

BELOW:
Podstakannik *tea glasses
in the CCCP restaurant,
Kiev, Ukraine.*

OPPOSITE:
*Men enjoying smoking a
narghile and drinking tea
in old Saida, Lebanon.*

RED TEA REACHES THE SHORES OF BRITAIN

BRITISH TEA: OXIDIZED, MILKY, AND FULL-BODIED

The first chests of tea from China were brought back by Dutch ships and unloaded in the port of London in 1645. The British developed a marked liking for oxidized teas, which they called black teas (known as red teas by the Chinese), and for the heavily oxidized Oolong teas to which they gave names such as "Oriental Beauty," "Fancy," and "Champagne." These teas, generally full-bodied, strong, and tannic, produce a dark and quite dense liquor. A number of theories have been put forward to explain the British liking for oxidized teas.

☞ A matter of geography: these were the types of tea produced in provinces close to the port of Canton, the only trading post accessible to Westerners until the mid-nineteenth century.

☞ A matter of flavor: the Western palate is not keen on bitterness, and as the oxidation process lessens this, it may well explain why these teas, more than any others, became popular in Europe – the addition of milk and sugar reducing the bitter taste still further.

☞ A matter of transportation: even though the tea was green when it left Canton, by the time it reached London it would have had time to "mature" and oxidize in the damp holds of the ships. Before the opening of the Suez Canal in 1869 and the introduction of steamships, merchant vessels took six months to sail from Canton to London.

A DRINK OF THE ARISTOCRACY AND OF THE WORKING CLASSES

As in every new country to which tea was introduced, it remained the preserve of the elite before eventually permeating all levels of society.

Tea drinking among the aristocracy

The first people to drink tea on a daily basis were the directors of the East India Company who would take a tea break in the afternoon, a sacred tradition in the world of British business. The East India Company was formed by Queen Elizabeth I to handle all trade with China, including the tea trade. It was one of the largest financial organizations of the time

with its headquarters in London and exercising influence all over the world. For 250 years the East India Company enjoyed a monopoly over the tea trade both in Europe and the states of America.

It was the Portuguese *infanta*, Catherine of Braganza, who introduced tea to the English court after her marriage to King Charles II in 1662. She had already enjoyed drinking tea in Portugal, no doubt thanks to the great Portuguese merchants who had a trading post in Macao.

A drink of the bourgeoisie: the introduction of tea rooms

Tea reached the middle classes via tea salons or tea rooms. One of the earliest was Tom's Coffee House founded by Sir Thomas Twining in the 1700s. Twining had the idea of serving and selling coffee and tea in coffee houses, which were at the time the exclusive reserve of men. He therefore opened a room where women could come to buy and drink tea without drawing public attention to themselves. At this period 3$^1/_2$ ounces (100 grams) of Chinese green gunpowder tea cost no less than the modest sum of \$184 (£150) in today's money. British tea houses hit on the idea of creating blends of teas of different origins to meet different tastes and requirements according to the time of day. This is how the English tea blends with their various names came into being, the blends themselves varying from one tea shop to another ("Morning Tea," "Brunch Tea," "Five o'clock Tea"). Additionally, certain famous blends were created in honor of the British royal family, including "Queen Victoria" and "Royal Morning Tea."

ABOVE, FROM LEFT TO RIGHT:
The quiet, cozy atmosphere of the Simple Simon English tea room in Lyons.

Collection of British teapots and mugs, and a coaster with a portrait of Princess Diana.

ABOVE:
*Afternoon tea at the Simple
Simon tea room, Lyons.*

OPPOSITE:
*Traditional afternoon tea
service.*

Pensioners' club enjoying
afternoon tea, England,
1938.

Afternoon tea

True "afternoon tea" did not appear until the nineteenth century and was introduced by Anna Russell, Duchess of Bedford (1783–1857).

Finding the period between lunch and dinner to be too long for her, she adopted the habit around four o'clock in the afternoon of having tea served in her rooms, accompanied by a light snack. It was she who started this new fashion of afternoon tea served in fine Chinese porcelain, accompanied by, for example, sandwiches, scones, and crumpets.

EARL GREY: A TRADITIONAL BRITISH TEA
The story goes that during a diplomatic visit to Canton, Earl Grey, foreign secretary for the British Crown in the early years of the nineteenth century, discovered a blend of Chinese tea and bitter orange peel in a tea house in the city. He considered this combination to be delicious and brought the recipe back with him to England.

Replacing the bitter orange with bergamot, he gave the recipe to a London firm who, out of gratitude, named the blend after him.

Tea drinking among the working classes: high tea

With the introduction of gas lighting around 1830, the working day grew longer. Breakfast was taken early in the morning, at midday a light snack sufficed, and dinner was eaten later, in the evening. In working-class communities, high tea gradually replaced dinner: this was eaten late in the afternoon, after the end of the working day. Tea was drunk in a simple, unsophisticated manner accompanied by potato cakes, meat, or haddock poached in milk, and by a dessert.

THE BIRTH OF THE MUG
At breakfast, a hot drink made from beer and warm milk known as posset was replaced by tea. Posset was drunk from tankards, and it was from the shape of these that the modern mug is derived. Some people enjoyed their morning tea accompanied by scrambled eggs while others even ate the tea leaves.

ABOVE, FROM LEFT TO RIGHT:
Hook in the shape of a teapot, and knitted kettle holder.

Advertisement for tea with an image of the British monarch Edward VII.

A cup of full-bodied English tea with milk.

BRITISH CONTROL OF THE TEA TRADE

Until the nineteenth century, when Britain freed itself from the Chinese monopoly on production, tea accounted for more than a third of the value of imports from China. Quantities rose from 14,000 short tons (12,700 metric tons) in 1720 to 400,000 short tons (360,000 metric tons) in 1830. To handle these vast tea imports, an auction room was opened in London in 1834 when the East India Company lost its monopoly. In its heyday it handled more than 75 percent of world production. The auction room finally closed its doors in 1998. Auction rooms still exist in the major tea-exporting countries such as India, Kenya, Sri Lanka, Malawi, Bangladesh, and Indonesia.

Opium war or tea war?

Recognizing an ever-increasing demand for tea, the Chinese began to supply a poorer-quality product at higher cost, selling their green gold for inflated prices. It was impossible for the British to get into China and see how the plant was cultivated: China tolerated trade with these "foreign barbarians" on condition that their presence was restricted to just one trading port, Canton. The British then tried to create demands among the Chinese that they could satisfy in exchange for tea. This began with cotton, which came from Britain's Indian colonies; then, at the end of the eighteenth century, they began exchanging opium produced in Bengal, which was transported and traded for tea via clandestine routes. It soon became the currency for which tea changed hands. In response, in 1839 the emperor declared the port of Canton closed to foreigners. The British sent in warships and China surrendered in 1842, acknowledging British superiority with the signing of the Treaty of Nanking, which stipulated a free trade in opium and the ceding of Hong Kong (which became a British commercial base).

TEA PRODUCTION IN THE BRITISH COLONIES

The introduction of tea to India

"The tea and flower route"

Keen to free itself from reliance on imports of Chinese tea, Britain sent a botanist, Robert Fortune, to China in 1848. Disguised as a Chinaman, he gained access to the tea plantations and brought back tea plants and tea seeds in his luggage. He was also accompanied by 85 Chinese tea experts.

The mountainous area around the town of Darjeeling provided ideal climatic conditions in which to develop plantations producing good-quality tea. Other suitable regions included the area of Assam to the east of Darjeeling, the Nilgiri and Anaimalai hills in southern India, and outlying regions such as Nepal and Sikkim.

The introduction of tea cultivation in India therefore dates from the second half of the nineteenth century. At this period and for more than a hundred years, only oxidized tea was produced. Indeed, it is only in the last ten years or so that certain tea gardens[8] have started to diversify.

Chinese tea began to take second place, and even became unpopular in Europe.

The supremacy of Darjeeling

Darjeeling teas rapidly began to sell for very high prices on the British market. The care taken in the management of the gardens, the picking, and mechanized production allowed them to compete with the best that China could produce. The number of tea gardens rose from 39 in 1866 to 113 in 1874. Today there are around a hundred gardens each covering tens of acres, but some gardens now cover almost 250 acres (approximately 100 hectares).

OPPOSITE, FROM TOP TO BOTTOM:
Tea plantation outside the town of Coonor in the Nilgiri Hills in southern India.

Tea pickers returning from different areas of the plantation line up to weigh the tea they have picked; they must pick a minimum quantity and may get a bonus according to the quality and for additional weight, Nuwara Eliya, Sri Lanka.

Freshly picked tea leaves from a fine harvest in Darjeeling, India.

[8] *"Garden" is the name given to a plantation or area of a plantation sharing the same conditions and aspect.*

Masala chai, *an everyday drink in India.*

BELOW:
Women drinking masala chai *while waiting in a store.*

OPPOSITE:
Old man wearing a lungi *(a long piece of cotton cloth traditionally worn by men) and sipping a glass of* masala chai *on the street.*

MASALA CHAI

MAKES 5 GLASSES OF TEA

$^1/_2$ TEASPOON OF MASALA TEA (A SPECIAL BLEND OF
GROUND SPICES FOR TEA SOLD IN INDIAN GROCERY
STORES)

2 TEASPOONS OF WHOLE-LEAF ASSAM TEA (THE DRY
LEAVES SHOULD BE STRONGLY AROMATIC WITH
DOMINANT TOBACCO AND FLORAL NOTES)

1 PINT/$^1/_2$ LITER OF WHOLE MILK

*Put the masala tea and Assam tea in the milk and
bring to a boil. Allow to simmer for 1 or 2
minutes, then remove from the heat and allow to
stand for 3 to 4 minutes. Strain the milk and pour
into glasses. Sugar can be added to taste and some
cardamom seeds placed in each glass for
decoration.*

"Bitter" Assam tea

During forest clearing on the plains of Assam
in northeast India, a wild variety of tea plant
was found that had not been used by the local
population; it was named *Camellia sinensis
assamica*. Much better acclimatized to the
plains of Assam than the Chinese variety
brought back by Robert Fortune, it was
domesticated and planted there during
the 1850s.

The deforestation of the Assam jungle in
order to plant tea was not without its human
costs. The poor conditions in the early years
required a more labor-intensive management
of the plantations, and Assam was soon
supplanted by Darjeeling. Today some fine teas
are produced with aromatic properties that are
the equal of the Darjeeling brand.

India becomes one of the largest tea-consuming countries

In the early years of the twentieth century,
although India was a major tea producer, very
little tea was consumed in the country itself.
The upper classes were quick to adopt the
English custom and slowly the habit spread to
the rest of the population.

Today, tea has become India's national
drink and 65 percent of its production
(though not the best quality) is consumed
within India itself. Originally planted by
foreigners purely for their own needs and
profit, tea has now become a key element of
the Indian economy and culture. Wherever
you go, there are countless stores and booths
where you can buy a glass of *masala chai* tea
(tea with a blend of spices). The tea used is
broken-leaf boiled in milk or water with
sugar (or sweetened evaporated milk) and a
blend of spices (such as pepper, cardamom,
cloves, and nutmeg).

The introduction of tea to Ceylon: the consequence of plant disease

Formerly known as Ceylon by the British, this
island off the southeast coast of India, which
became Sri Lanka in 1972, was once a major
coffee producer. The collapse of coffee prices
during the 1850s due to the development of the
Brazilian coffee industry and the devastation
caused by the pathogen *Hemileia vastatrix*
(coffee-leaf rust) put an end to the island's
coffee plantations within 30 years. By 1890, not
a single coffee plant remained on the island.
Some forward-looking plantation owners
began planting tea as a replacement crop and
in just a few years the island was completely
dominated by this newcomer, which adapted
perfectly to the climatic conditions of Sri
Lanka's central highlands.

Thomas Lipton, a wealthy Irish businessman who had
started out as a grocer, first moved into tea in Sri Lanka in
the 1890s, buying up former coffee plantations cheaply
and setting about producing tea in the Uva region of the
island. He adopted an American-style commercial
approach to relaunch a drink that he had already been
selling in his stores as a luxury item. By producing the tea
himself, Lipton was able to lower his production costs and
popularize this exotic drink, which until then had been
out of the reach of the middle classes. With his slogan
"direct from the tea garden to the teapot," he succeeded in
transforming Sri Lankan tea into the island's "green gold"
and won himself worldwide fame in the process.

The development of tea cultivation in East and Central Africa

Kenya was the first country in Africa to
produce tea and is currently the world's fourth-
largest producer. Tea was introduced into
Kenya by the British immediately after World
War I. Some major English firms remain
firmly installed in the country and still control
more than 9,900 acres (about 4,000 hectares) to
the east of Lake Victoria.

Other African countries followed including
Malawi, Uganda, Tanzania, and Zimbabwe,
which are among the largest tea producers on
the continent of Africa.

In all these "new" producer countries –
whether it be India, Sri Lanka, Indonesia, or
the countries of Africa – it is almost impossible
to find good tea to drink because the best-
quality teas are destined for export.

A SOUTH AFRICAN TEA THAT IS NOT TEA:
ROOIBOS OR REDBUSH "TEA"
In many languages, no distinction is made between tea
and infusion; hence the confusion between plants that are
infused in the same way as tea, and genuine tea that
comes from the *Camellia sinensis* plant.

In South Africa, a plant known as "rooibos" or
"redbush" tea is cultivated that is not, in fact, tea at all.
The plant, which has the botanical name *Aspalathus
linearis*, contains no theine (caffeine) and is very low in
tannins. This red "tea" infusion was introduced at the
beginning of the twentieth century. A highly refreshing
drink, it soon became very popular and, by the 1930s,
plantations were being developed in the Cederberg
region 155 miles (250 kilometers) north of Cape Town.
Branches of this plant are harvested during the summer
and part of the fall, and finely chopped. They are then
left to ferment for 8 to 24 hours, and dried in the sun
before being packaged.

ABOVE, FROM LEFT TO
RIGHT:
*Sir Thomas Lipton, an
important figure in the
popularization of tea,
which became the national
drink of the British (1900
portrait).*

*Hédiard company tea chest
from India.*

FOLLOWING DOUBLE PAGE:
*Plantation in the Nuwara
Eliya region, Sri Lanka,
where the former factory
has been converted into a
hotel known as the* Tea
Factory. *A minifactory
continues to produce tea
for the hotel, which is
always well stocked with
fresh tea.*

TEAS OF THE AMERICAS

The development of tea cultivation in South America

North America and Canada, like Europe, have been major consumers of tea since the seventeenth century. To meet their needs, they developed plantations in South America during the course of the twentieth century. The two principal tea-producing countries are Argentina and Brazil, which produce mainly broken-leaf teas used as a raw material for tea derivatives such as tea bags, iced tea and freeze-dried tea, manufactured in the United States of America.

MATÉ: A SOUTH AMERICAN PLANT

Maté is a plant that originated in Paraguay and is rich in mateine – an alkaloid with a formula very similar to theine (caffeine); its botanical name is *Ilex paraguariensis*. It was originally consumed by the Guarani tribe of Paraguay to promote vitality, health, and longevity. In the seventeenth century the Jesuits recognized its properties, and began cultivating the plant and encouraging its cultivation and consumption in Argentina and Brazil. It became known as *yerba maté* or "Jesuits' elixir." Then, in the nineteenth century, the gauchos of Argentina made it their own, drinking it every day and introducing the custom of sipping it from a gourd through a strainer straw. Locally it is still far more widely drunk than tea.

Maté grows in the Amazon forest. The most tender leaves are picked and broken before being exposed to high temperatures to destroy the enzymes responsible for oxidation of the leaves. The leaves are then smoked for a day over a wood fire, which is what gives maté its characteristic taste. The leaves are then dried completely and, unlike tea, left for between six months and two years before being used to allow their full flavor to develop. It makes a delicious drink, both piping hot and iced, and can be mixed with other plants, such as citronella, sage, and mint.

In perfumery, what is referred to as a "tea" note is in fact maté absolute.

North American inventions

The birth of iced tea

Iced tea was invented in the United States in 1904 at the St. Louis World's Fair, which took place in the summer. That summer had been particularly hot, and a tea seller called Richard Blechynden was finding it difficult to attract customers to the booth where he was serving piping-hot tea. He hit on the idea of adding ice cubes to the tea. It was an immediate success, and iced tea was born.

The birth of the tea bag

During the second decade of the twentieth century, Thomas Sullivan, a New York tea and coffee importer, decided to promote his range of teas by distributing them in small quantities. He packaged the tea in small silk sachets, which were soon replaced by gauze. This was how the tea bag was born, though it later evolved into a paper sachet containing powdered tea. During recent years there has been a return to quality tea in bags, with whole-leaf tea sold in muslin bags, combining practicality with quality.

THE PERFECT ICED TEA

It is important to steep the tea in water at room temperature, not hot water. Place two teaspoons of tea in 2 pints (1 liter) of water at about 68°F/20°C. Leave to infuse for between 20 and 45 minutes, depending on the type of tea and according to taste (allow less time for green teas than for Oolong and red teas). Citrus peel, spices, sugar, or honey may be added if desired. Strain the tea and place in the refrigerator. Drink within 24 hours.

The best teas to drink as iced teas are, of course, aromatized teas or flower teas, but you can also use plain teas such as Japanese green teas, red teas from China, Sri Lanka, or Assam, and Oolong teas.

GREEN TEA OPENS A NEW GATEWAY TO AFRICA

THE INTRODUCTION OF GREEN TEA TO MOROCCO: A SYRUPY, TANGY DRINK

In Morocco and sub-Saharan Africa, tea forms part of the collective consciousness with the sense that tea drinking is an age-old tradition, whereas in fact it is only a relatively recent introduction. Tea drinking in these countries dates back to the eighteenth century and became increasingly popular toward the end of the nineteenth century. It enjoyed rapid success among Moroccans, who were already drinking infusions of various other plants. Tea, with its beneficial properties, therefore came as a welcome addition.

OPPOSITE:
Women traders selling fresh mint for tea on the streets of Bamako, Mali.

A traditional tea set as used in the Sahara and sub-Saharan regions of Africa; it consists of two enameled metal teapots, one for making the tea, the other for serving it; Bandiagara, Mali.

The eighteenth century: a royal ritual

Sultan Moulay Ismael (1672–1727) was one of the first to discover the drink. Tea was among the gifts presented to him by various British and Dutch delegations, and he was quick to appreciate it, particularly for its health-giving properties.

As soon as tea drinking was introduced in Morocco, it became ritualized. The preparation of the tea was the responsibility of the *moul atai* or "tea man." Two trays were brought: one with tea glasses and two teapots; the other with caddies of tea, various plant leaves including mint, loaf sugar (and a hammer with which to break it), and a vial of orange-blossom water. The water was kept hot in a kettle over a brazier. A servant was then ordered to prepare the tea, which he did sitting cross-legged. The two teapots, containing amounts of similar strength, were poured simultaneously, filling the glasses with a uniform blend and balancing the two infusions. The tea was poured from a height to aerate the liquid and produce a foam on the top. Dishes of cakes or dried fruit were served to accompany the tea.

The nineteenth century: a ritual of the urban elite that permeated society

Until the end of the nineteenth century, the ceremony associated with drinking mint tea remained the privilege of the urban bourgeoisie. It was the master of the house who presided, the tea always being prepared in front of the guests following the same ritual as that of the sultan. Tea was served in order of precedence according to age and social rank,

and the guests drank with noisy inhalations to indicate that the tea was delicious. Once the first glass of tea had been consumed, the master of the house prepared a second, and then a third. His guest was obliged to drink them all, as failure to do so was considered rude. The three stages of hospitality:

The first glass is bitter, like life.
The second is as sweet as love.
The third is as soothing as death.

ARAB PROVERB.

At the end of the nineteenth century, tea made the transition from being the drink of the elite to a drink enjoyed by the people. After the Crimean War, England, which at that time enjoyed a monopoly in the tea trade with Europe and America, and was looking for new markets, flooded the Moroccan market with Chinese green tea. The consumption of this tea slowly permeated through all the strata of Moroccan society, from the well-off urban dwellers to the rural population. Other aromatic plants were added to enhance the tea according to season and region. In winter, wormwood was often added; in fall and spring, verbena and sage; and basil in summer. In the Atlas Mountains, tea was drunk with rosemary and wild thyme.

NORTH MOROCCAN MINT TEA: SWEET AND AROMATIC

1 TEASPOON OF CHINESE GUNPOWDER OR HYSON GREEN TEA
1 LARGE BUNCH OF FRESH MINT
4 TO 6 SUGAR CUBES
1 SMALL TEAPOT (11 FLUID OUNCES/ 33 CENTILITERS) AND 4 TEA GLASSES

Bring fresh water to a boil. Put the tea in the teapot. Pour on boiling water, rinse around the pot, then pour the water away. Add the mint and then the sugar. Fill the teapot with boiling water. Leave to stand for 1 or 2 minutes, then pour the tea from the teapot into a glass and from the glass back into the teapot, continuing this process until you think that the ingredients are fully blended. Prepare two more rounds of tea with the same tea leaves, adding sugar and mint. You can also add some drops of orange-blossom water to each glass. In winter, a few wormwood leaves in the bottom of the glass will enhance the aroma of the tea. Tip: to achieve a good infusion, the water must be boiling, not simmering, contrary to usual advice.

ABOVE:
Woman preparing mint tea in the traditional manner, Pâtisserie Tesnime, Paris.

OPPOSITE, FROM TOP TO BOTTOM:
Man selling fresh mint, Morocco.

Woman spreading out filo pastry to make pastries, Pâtisserie Tesnime, Paris.

Pastries to accompany mint tea, Pâtisserie Tesnime, Paris.

Tea glasses and teapots, Pâtisserie Tesnime, Paris.

ACROSS THE SAHARA: A FULL-BODIED, PUNGENT BREW

Tuaregs preparing their pungent, full-bodied tea in the Sahara.

Tea began its journey across the Sahara to sub-Saharan Africa at the end of the nineteenth century with Berber nomads. For the peoples of the Sahara, tea is one of the three drinks essential to life in the desert: "Water is life, milk is survival, and tea is the national drink." As one heads further south, the tea becomes fuller-bodied; mint is no longer used and the tea is often "cooked" with camel milk and sugar, giving it a caramel color and a full-bodied, pungent flavor. Two teapots are used: one to "cook" the tea, the other to serve it.

Three things are needed in order to make tea: time, hot charcoal, and friends.

Tuareg proverb.

Tea continued its journey southward in Africa throughout the twentieth century. However, it was not until the 1970s that the people of southern Mali began to drink tea regularly, though it had been consumed in the north of the country for some time before.

A well-made glass of tea
should have a layer of
foam on top.

CONTACT WITH THE WEST BRINGS THE AROMATIZATION OF TEA

THE ADVENT OF GOURMET TEAS

The aromatization of tea has its origins in China. Since the time of the Tang dynasty, the Chinese had been accustomed to perfuming certain teas with flower petals and enhancing tea infusions with spices, aromatic plants, and citrus peel. A distinction is made between perfumed teas and aromatized teas. The latter are aromatized by spraying the tea leaves with essential oils, whereas perfumed teas are fragranced with flower petals and spices.

Tea with flowers, perfumed teas

In China, teas have been perfumed with flowers since the Tang period. Certain flowers harmonize better with certain tea colors. Generally speaking, jasmine (*Jasminum sambac* or *Jasminum paniculatum*) is used with white or green teas, rose and gardenia with Oolong and red teas, osmanthus (sweet olive) with roasted Oolong teas, and orange and plum blossom with red teas.

These combinations are only possible in places where tea plantations and the required flowers grow together in close proximity. It is the freshness of each ingredient that produces the subtle and perfect marriage of flavors. Furthermore, good-quality raw materials — that is to say, high-quality tea and high-quality flower petals — are needed.

The region that specializes in the finest-quality jasmine teas is Fujian province in China.

The tea is harvested in September, the optimum period for picking jasmine. Both tea leaves and jasmine buds are gathered at dawn. Once the green tea has been "fixed" by exposure to heat, it is brought into contact with the freshly picked jasmine buds. Between 60 and 100 lbs (30 to 50 kilos) of flowers are needed for 200 lbs (100 kilos) of undried tea leaves. Fine layers of tea leaves are alternated with fine layers of petals to produce a carpet an inch or so thick. The tea leaves, which are still humid, easily absorb all the aromas and capture the fragrance of the jasmine. The mixture is left to stand under a thatch covering for 24 hours and then heated for an hour before removing the flowers, which would otherwise give a bitterness to the infusion.

A fine-quality jasmine tea is necessarily very expensive, given the quantity of flowers needed to perfume the tea. Originally it was medium-quality teas that were improved in this way but it later became a veritable art form, particularly in the case of jasmine, with *grand cru* tea leaves being used to produce delicately perfumed teas. Commercially, one mainly finds cheap jasmine teas that have been aromatized with artificial aromas and often with the addition of quantities of jasmine flowers, whose purpose is purely decorative.

Aromatized teas

The boom in the Western food-processing industry in the late 1960s with the introduction of flavored fruit juices had positive effects on the aromatization of tea. The first aromatized teas were based on the aromas of our domestic fruits, before more exotic varieties were sought out. The fashion today is for blends of aromas with evocative names suggesting far-flung destinations.

One positive repercussion of the introduction of gourmet, fruity teas has been the revival of the image of tea itself. In the West, tea had suffered from an antiquated and overly feminine image. The advent of this new family of teas gave the drink a more modern and contemporary image, which gradually helped to reestablish its reputation with the Western consumer. There are many tea drinkers who begin by drinking flavored teas and gradually move in the direction of the more subtle quality teas once their palate has been "educated." This type of tea was also the first in Europe to be used by chocolate makers and chefs. As the aromas in flavored teas are stronger and more pronounced, they were easier to use than (nonaromatized) origin teas, but there was a loss of subtlety.

Although for purists such teas cannot be described as "true" teas, creating perfumed blends is nevertheless an art in its own right. In fact, just as when making a good Kir, the raw ingredients must themselves be of good quality in order to produce a harmonious blend in which the tea notes and aromas combine and complement without either stifling the other. Every tea merchant's has its secret, home-made recipes with names evoking travel, places, seasons, and historical figures.

ABOVE:
Loose tea packaged in tins by tea importers, France.

FOLLOWING DOUBLE PAGE:
Tea warehouse belonging to Dammann Frères, one of the oldest tea importers in France.

ABOVE LEFT:
Old ink stamps for marking aromatized tea bags, Kusmi Tea, Paris.

ABOVE RIGHT:
Lithogravure plates for tea caddies, Dammann Frères, Orgeval.

OPPOSITE:
Darjeeling and Yunnan teas.

AROMATIZATION TECHNIQUES

The aromas used can be "nature-identical" – that is to say, manufactured by the chemical industry but derived from molecules that exist in nature – or they can be artificial.

Any type of tea – white, green, Oolong, red, or black – can be aromatized by spraying essential oils onto the tea leaves. As this is done onto dry, processed leaves, aromatization is usually carried out in the consumer country rather than the producer country.

Flower petals or fruit peel may also be added for decoration and to give the infusion more body. *Hibiscus sabdariffa* (red sorrel), a plant used a great deal in infusions in some countries, brings a fresh, acid note when mixed with tea and gives the liquor a strikingly beautiful pink-red color.

II ALCHEMY OF TEA

TEA IS A PRODUCT THAT DEPENDS ON LOCAL CONDITIONS. CLIMATE, ASPECT, AND SOIL PLAY AN IMPORTANT ROLE IN ENABLING THE YOUNG LEAVES AND BUDS TO DEVELOP THEIR DELICATE FLAVORS. IT IS THE CAREFUL PROCESSING CARRIED OUT BY HUMAN BEINGS THAT TRANSFORMS THESE FRESH YOUNG SHOOTS FROM THEIR ORIGINAL GREEN TO THE SIX DIFFERENT COLORS OR TEA FAMILIES: WHITE, GREEN, YELLOW, BLUE-GREEN, RED, AND BLACK. THE CHEMICAL COMPOSITION OF TEA ALSO GIVES IT BENEFICIAL QUALITIES THAT HAVE BEEN RECOGNIZED AND USED BY HUMANS FOR CENTURIES.

AGRONOMY: FROM PLANT TO CUP

THE DEMANDING YET GENEROUS NATURE OF THE TEA PLANT

The tea plant: a camellia

The tea plant is a member of the Theaceae family. It is a *Camellia* of the species *sinensis* (which means "from China"). It arrived from Asia at the end of the sixteenth century and became known in Europe at the same period as its cousins, the ornamental camellias, *Camellia japonica* and *Camellia sasanqua*, but in the form of dry leaves, never in the form of a living plant for cultivation. The Chinese soon recognized the economic advantage of the tea plant as a drink and did everything they could to conceal from the West for as long as possible how tea was produced. The particular feature of the *sinensis* species is that, unlike other camellias, its foliage is very rich in aromatic compounds.

Two varieties, "sinensis" and "assamica," are now grown on five continents, except in China and Japan where the "sinensis" variety continues to be the only variety cultivated. The "assamica" variety was discovered much

later, in the nineteenth century, when the British began clearing the forests of the Assam region to grow tea plants from China. They discovered this new tea plant variety by chance and went on to domesticate it, initially introducing it to their plantations in Assam, realizing that the "assamica" variety was much better suited to the plains of Assam than was the "sinensis" variety.

The "sinensis" variety of *Camellia sinensis* is a mountain plant that is more aromatic and less productive than the "assamica" variety of *Camellia sinensis*, which is more robust and cultivated mainly on the plains. All the plantations established by Westerners include a variable percentage of "assamica" and "sinensis," the real skill being to achieve a balance between productivity and gustatory qualities. For example, in the mountain region of Darjeeling, 75 percent of tea plants grown in each plantation are of the "sinensis" variety and 25 percent "assamica," whereas on the plains of Assam, over 90 percent of tea plants are of the "assamica" variety.

There are hybrids derived from these two varieties as well as many subvarieties of "sinensis," particularly ecotypes, that is to say, sub varieties that have appeared through adaptation to a specific "terroir" or locality

over the centuries. This is the case with tea plants in Japan, which originally derived from the "sinensis" variety introduced to the archipelago in the twelfth century: over more than eight centuries of cultivation, this nonindigenous variety has developed specific morphological and aromatic characteristics that distinguish it from the original "sinensis" variety.

The age of a tea plant is also a factor that influences taste: the older it is, the more complex and subtle are its aromatic qualities. In certain plantations in China and Japan, there are tea plants known to be several centuries old. In the plantations developed by the Europeans, such as those in India, Sri Lanka, and Kenya, some tea plants date back to those originally planted and are therefore more than 150 years old. The average life of a tea plant is about 50 years. After a new tea bush is planted, there is a two-year delay before harvesting can begin. Stem training is practiced to encourage the tea plant to produce more branches while yet remaining small – no taller than 4 feet (1.2 meters) – making it easier to harvest, whereas in its wild state the tea plant can grow to more than 20 feet (6 meters) in height. These stems are trained to form a "picking table." Between each harvesting

period the bushes are lightly clipped to encourage the growth of the plant for the following period. To bring new vigor to the plant and restrict its height and width, every four to five years a more severe pruning known as production pruning is carried out, leaving only the trunk and a few of the larger branches.

The impact of "terroir"

Climate

Tea plants grow at their best in tropical and subtropical regions. Hardy and adaptable, their cultivation has been extended into temperate climates such as that of northern Turkey, Georgia, the Azores, and even Italy, between 43° north and 33° south. Although tea can withstand frost, it prefers a warm climate, with average temperatures of around 66°F (19°C); humidity, with an annual rainfall of over 60 inches (1,500 millimeters) (in France it is about 30 inches (750 millimeters); a daily minimum of five hours of more or less direct sunshine; and nights that are relatively cool.

TEA PLANTS IN THE SHADE

In Japan, certain high-quality spring teas are grown in the shade so that the leaves remain very tender and rich in specific aromatic compounds. Entire plantations are covered with roofing made of rice straw or large black sheets a few weeks before harvesting. *Gyokuro* is a tea that receives this treatment, developing a very particular smoothness and sweetness, unlike the *sencha* tea grown in the same area in open sunlight, which produces a much sharper tea.

Two sorts of the powdered *maccha* tea are produced: *usucha*, which is used to make a light tea, and *koicha* for strong tea. *Usucha* comes from young tea plants that are covered just three weeks before harvesting, while *koicha* comes from old tea plants that have always been grown in the shade. *Koicha* tea is fuller-bodied but also smoother than *usucha*.

Altitude

Altitude is another determining factor in tea production, as it produces warm, sunny days and cool, damp nights: ideal conditions for concentrating the aromas found in tea. Tea bushes are therefore cultivated as high as 10,000 feet (3,000 meters) above sea level.

ALTITUDE AND CONCENTRATION OF AROMAS

Sri Lanka has three major tea-growing areas of different altitudes.
☞ The "low-grown" plantations: from sea level to 2,000 feet (0 to 600 meters), accounting for 35 percent of the land. These fast-growing tea plants usually produce a dark, bland, sweetish liquor. They are used for blending.
☞ The "medium-grown" plantations: from 2,000 to 4,300 feet (600 to 1,300 meters), accounting for 25 percent of the land. The tea from this altitude is of medium quality, woody, and low in astringency.
☞ The "high-grown" plantations: above 4,300 feet (1,300 meters), accounting for 40 percent of the land. These are the most highly prized teas as they grow far more slowly, producing high-quality teas with sharp, concentrated aromas very similar to certain Darjeelings.

Latitude

Harvesting periods are, to a large extent, determined by the proportions of daylight and darkness over a 24-hour period, and therefore by latitude. In all regions situated above 16° south and north, where tea plants are exposed for more than six weeks to less than 11 hours 15 minutes of daylight, they enter dormancy, that is to say, their growth slows down. As a result, harvesting stops. This period runs from the end of fall to the end of winter. However, in latitudes below 16°, closer to the equator, tea can be harvested throughout the year.

The dormancy phase is important, as when the tea plant begins growing again in the spring, the young shoots secrete aromatic compounds that give a characteristic flavor not

found in later harvests. The countries best known for their spring teas are China, Japan, and the Darjeeling and Assam regions of northern India, all situated above 20° north.

On the other hand, in southern India, Sri Lanka, Indonesia, and Kenya – which are among the world's major tea producers – harvesting continues throughout the year as they are all situated between 20° north and south.

A TEA FOR EACH SEASON

In Darjeeling each tea garden produces four harvests.

☞ The spring harvest begins end February/beginning March, continuing into April. A light pruning is done to encourage the tea plants to regenerate over three weeks.

☞ The summer harvest, which then begins, continues from mid-May to mid-June.

☞ The monsoon harvest takes place during July and August. Some gardens do not pick during this warm, rainy season as the teas produced are very light, bitter, and low in aromatics. These teas are often disposed of on the local market in the form of broken leaves.

☞ The fall harvest runs from mid-September to the end of October. A light pruning is then done. After this, the tea plant enters dormancy for over four months, from the end of October to the end of February.

The spring teas produce a yellow-green liquor that is slightly bitter and astringent with dominant plant and white flower notes. The summer and fall teas are fuller-bodied and less sharp, sometimes developing fruity Muscat notes.

In Japan there are also four harvests.

☞ The spring harvest, or *ichiban-cha*: from mid-April to the beginning of May, accounting for half the total harvest.

☞ The summer harvest, or *niban-cha*: from mid-June to the beginning of July. Then, during the hot, humid summer season, the tea plants are left unpicked as the tea is not good.

☞ The late summer harvest, or *sanban-cha*: from the end of August to the beginning of September.

☞ The fall harvest, or *yoban-cha*: from the end of September to the beginning of October. This is discretionary, depending on the weather conditions that year.

Between each harvest, a light pruning is done to encourage growth. The plants are then left to regenerate for at least two weeks.

In Sri Lanka, tea is picked throughout the year, as the tea plants are in constant production and do not enter dormancy. Other factors play their part in the quality of the tea harvested, in particular the exposure of the hillsides to the monsoon.

☞ Plantations on slopes with a southwest aspect – which are exposed to the monsoon coming from the southwest from May to August – are known for their winter teas produced from December to March.

☞ Plantations on slopes with a northeast aspect – which are exposed to the monsoon coming from the northeast from October to January – are known for the teas produced from May to September.

ABOVE, FROM LEFT TO RIGHT:
Tea picking in the mists of the Nilgiri Hills, southern India; the climate, with days of alternating mist and bright spells, is well suited to the cultivation of tea bushes. The wooden pole resting on the bushes acts as a level so that the tea picker plucks only the newest shoots.

Tea plants have a long taproot allowing them to root deeply in the soil and draw on the nutrients and characteristic elements of each type of soil, the "very substance" of the earth.

BELOW:
Tea factory near Ooty, Tamil Nadu, India.

FOLLOWING DOUBLE PAGE:
Tea plantation in Sri Lanka with tree cover acting as a wind break. The dark-green areas are where the tea has been harvested and the pale-green areas are where it is yet to be picked (the young shoots are a fluorescent green).

Soil

Both "sinensis" and "assamica" tea varieties thrive on acid soils that are quite sandy and well drained, and contain a good layer of humus. In Darjeeling and the Nilgiri and Anaimalai hills in India, in Sri Lanka, and in certain regions of Japan, tea plants flourish on acid, sedentary soils produced by the erosion of the gneiss or granite mother rock. In the Assam region of northeast India, tea is cultivated on acid, alluvial soils. In Kenya, Indonesia, and certain regions of Japan, tea plantations are on acid soils rich in volcanic ash. The same variety of tea grown on two different soil types will produce different results. The Chinese understood this very early on: there are writings dating from as early as the eleventh century that refer to the notion of local conditions (or "terroir") – in other words, the role of soil and aspect in a single tea garden covering a few acres (see "A question of 'terroir'" below). Trials are still being carried out to try to discover new characteristics in teas grown in one country or another, or in one region or another within the same country. For example, Taiwanese "sinensis" subvarieties were introduced to Darjeeling in India to produce blue-green teas; "sinensis" subvarieties of Chinese Mao Feng green teas were introduced to Chinese Keemun estates to produce red teas with a flowery note almost nonexistent in the local variety.

A QUESTION OF "TERROIR"
In a Chinese register dating from 1064, known as the *Dongxi Tea Tasters' Register* (*Dongxi shi cha lu*), the following comments are found concerning different places in the same Dongxi tea garden near the Wu-i mountains) (Wuyi Shan) in Fujian province.
"Heyuan: the tea grows on the north slope of the mountain; its taste is sweet and aromatic; its color greenish-white.
Hellingwei: the tea growing there is a yellow color and its taste is strongly reminiscent of the earth.
Likeng: the tea is yellow in color and its taste is short-lived.
Fowling, in Hekou: the tea is yellowish-white and its taste is short-lived.
Southeast of Fowling: the tea has little sweetness and is very bitter.
Northeast of Fowling: the taste is short-lived and the aroma lacks intensity." [1]

ORGANICALLY GROWN TEA
The tea plant is a perennial, usually grown on its own in areas with regular rainfall. This gradually leads to soil exhaustion through leaching, and a decrease in productivity despite the addition of chemical fertilizers. Over the last ten years in many plantations, first in India with other countries following, there has been a switch to organic farming. It takes two years before participating plantations can be certified organic. Weeding is prohibited, and only organic fertilizers and "natural" insecticides may be used. A very strict and precise set of requirements governs the entire supply chain, from producer to distributor; only then can the organic label be affixed to the tea packet, which must be marketed under seal.

The fineness of the plucking

The last stage out in the fields, which is crucial to the quality of the final product, is the fineness of the plucking. It is the fresh, young, jade-green shoots that are picked, as they are rich in aromatic compounds and have a balance of supple tannins giving power and body to the liquor without producing any unpleasant astringency.

With high-quality teas, only the bud and the first two leaves are picked. In premium harvests, only the bud is picked.

To produce 2.2 lbs (1 kilo) of dry tea, it takes on average 13.2 lbs (6 kilos) of fresh tea, or 12,000 young shoots (the first two leaves and the bud).

After picking, at the end of the harvesting season, the tea plants are pruned back quite hard to prepare them for the following season. When the British became involved in the production of red tea in India in the 1850s, they introduced a classification system for red teas based on the part of the plant harvested (with or without the bud, plus the next two or three leaves), on maturity (young shoots or shoots that are already long and mature), and on the condition of the shoot (whole or broken). This was in order to standardize tea as a product for export. This classification is still used today by all countries producing oxidized teas that have come under some degree of British influence.

[1] *From* Asie: savourer, goûter (Asia: Savor, Taste)*, volume III, article by Marco Ceresa, editor Flora Blanchon, PUF, 1995.*

From plantation to factory. The bud plus two leaves still on the plant.

Factory at the Labookellie garden, Sri Lanka; the storys of rooms where the tea is withered are well ventilated to speed up the dehydration process. When you are near the factory there is a characteristic smell – a delicious blend of Granny Smith apples, fresh grass, and jasmine.

BRITISH TEA CLASSIFICATION BY GRADE: OXIDIZED TEAS (EXCLUDING CHINESE TEAS)

OP is the basic grade; it consists only of leaves and is an abbreviation of Orange Pekoe. Orange here does not mean that the tea is flavored with orange; rather it is a term used in honor of the name of the Dutch royal family: Oranje Nassau. The word "Pekoe" is derived from the Chinese *pak-ho*, which means "fine down." The more letters a grade has, the greater the number and the younger the buds it contains and the younger, and hence smaller, the leaves.

Whole leaf
SFTGFOP1: Special Finest Tippy Golden Flowery Orange Pekoe no. 1.
→ Tea produced from a fine plucking (bud and two leaves) of very young, very small shoots. This grade is found mainly in spring harvests in Darjeeling.

SFTGFOP: Special Finest Tippy Golden Flowery Orange Pekoe.
→ Like SFTGFOP1 but with a higher proportion of more mature, and therefore longer, shoots.

FTGFOP: Finest Tippy Golden Flowery Orange Pekoe.
→ Like SFTGFOP but with more mature buds.

TGFOP: Tippy Golden Flowery Orange Pekoe.
→ A blend of approximately 50 percent fine plucking and 50 percent leaf-only.

GFOP: Golden Flowery Orange Pekoe.
→ Like TGFOP but with a lower proportion of fine plucking. This is a grade often found in fine quality teas grown in Assam.

FOP: Flowery Orange Pekoe.
→ Like TGFOP but with a smaller proportion of fine plucking, and therefore very few buds.

OP: Orange Pekoe.
→ Leaf-only plucking, no buds. This grade is often found in Sri Lanka, Kenya, and Indonesia.

Broken leaf (or broken)
TGFBOP: Tippy Golden Flowery Broken Orange Pekoe
TGBOP: Tippy Golden Broken Orange Pekoe
GFBOP: Golden Flowery Broken Orange Pekoe
FBOP: Flowery Broken Orange Pekoe
GBOP: Golden Broken Orange Pekoe
BOP: Broken Orange Pekoe

Fannings (from the verb *to fan*)
The fannings are the tea produced by sieving broken-leaf tea. There are no subcategories for this type of grade. The advantage of these teas is that they infuse quickly, producing a characteristic, strongly colored liquor, making them suitable for tea bags.

Dust
The dust is produced by a finer sieving of broken-leaf tea. Like fannings, dust is used to fill tea bags.

Fair trade tea

Most tea is produced in developing countries where labor is cheap and working conditions do not always meet human rights and environmental standards. More and more tea brands are now choosing to sell some of their produce under the "fair trade" standard.

Fair trade forms part of sustainable development that rests on three pillars: economic, social, and environmental.

"Sustainable development is development that meets the needs of the present without compromising the ability of future generations to meet their own needs."[2]

"Fair trade is a trading partnership, based on dialogue, transparency, and respect, that seeks greater equity in international trade.

It contributes to sustainable development by offering better trading conditions to, and securing the rights of, marginalized producers and workers – especially in the South."[3]

Under the "fair trade" approach, a contract is entered into between an importer or manufacturer, an accreditation organization and a producers' cooperative, under which a marketing chain is set up that will help producers by guaranteeing them an assured minimum price and improved working and living conditions. The accreditation body regularly inspects the whole chain from production to marketing to ensure that the specifications agreed by each contractor are met.

ABOVE, FROM LEFT TO RIGHT:
Harvested tea being brought in for weighing at the Kericho plantation, Kenya.

Tea brought in for weighing at a Darjeeling garden in India before being sent to the factory for processing.

[2] *Gro Harlem Brundtland was chair of the World Commission on Environment and Development appointed by the United Nations General Assembly in 1983. Her report,* Our Common Future, *published in 1987, is one of the founding documents of sustainable development and served as a basis for the first Earth Summit in Rio in 1992.*

[3] *FINE: a grouping including Fairtrade Labelling Organizations Inernational, the International Federation for Alternative Trade, the Network of European Worldshops, and the European Fair Trade Association.*

COMPOSITION OF A FRESH TEA LEAF

Compounds	% Dry matter[4]	Properties
Polyphenols (or tannins)	27 – 44	Smoothness, power, astringency, bitterness dependent on the polyphenols (their size, structure, and so on).
1) Flavanols: in oxidized (red) tea, flavanols complex to form large molecules: thearubigins and theaflavins (resulting from the polymerization of EGCG and EGC or ECG or EC).	19 – 33	Powerful antioxidants (theaflavins: antioxidants 4 to 5 times more powerful than vitamins C or E). Infusion is coppery in color (in red tea due to the presence of thearubigins and theaflavins).
→ epigallocatechin gallate (EGCG)	8 – 12	Antioxidant 5 times more powerful than vitamins C or E.
→ epicatechin gallate (ECG)	3 – 6	Polymerizes with EGCG during oxidation.
→ epigallocatechin (EGC)	3 – 6	Polymerizes with EGCG during oxidation.
→ epicatechin (EC)	1 – 3	Polymerizes with EGCG during oxidation.
→ catechin	1 – 2	Antioxidant twice as powerful as vitamins C or E.
→ gallocatechin	3 – 4	...
2) Flavonols (quercetin, campherol, myrecetin)	3 – 4	Quercetin: antioxidant 5 times more powerful than vitamins C or E; anti-inflammatory.
3) Anthocyanins	1 – 2	Pigment.
4) Phenolic acids	3 – 4	Astringency and bitterness.
Alkaloids	3 – 5	...
→ theine (caffeine) chemical name: trimethylxanthine	3 – 4	Bitterness. Stimulates the central nervous system; lipolytic.
→ theobromine	0.2	Powerful diuretic.
→ theophylline	0.5	Respiratory stimulant (used in asthma medication).
Protids	18 – 22	...
→ amino acids: including theanine (5-N-ethylglutamine) only found in the tea plant	3 – 4	Theanine combined with theine (caffeine) has relaxing and energizing properties.
→ proteins	14 – 17	Their breakdown plays a major role in the formation of aromatic compounds.
Organic acids including vitamin C	0.5 – 0.6	Tea processing destroys vitamin C.
Glucids	32 – 44	Not all glucids pass into the water during infusion, except for monosaccharides.
→ monosaccharides	4 – 5	Sugary taste but very low level.
→ polysaccharides	14 – 20	...
→ cellulose and hemicellulose	4 – 7	...
→ pectins	5 – 6	...
→ lignins	5 – 6	...
Lipids	3 – 5	Lipids are present at very low levels and do not pass easily into the water, making tea a drink low in calories (2 kcal/cup).
Chlorophylls	0.5 – 0.6	Pigment.
Mineral salts including fluorine, potassium, calcium, and magnesium	5 – 6	Fluorine action (helps to combat tooth decay) combined with the effects of polyphenols. No sodium: tea can therefore be consumed by those on a salt-free diet.
Volatile substances more than 600 identified	0.01 – 0.02	Form part of the aromas.

[4] To quantify the constituents of a fresh tea leaf, the dry material is analyzed – that is, an abstraction is made of the roughly 90 percent water of which its weight is composed. The percentages shown in this table have been calculated in this way.

THE SIX COLORS OF TEA:
A QUESTION OF OXIDATION

The six tea colors were created in China under the Ming dynasty (1368–1644). They correspond to different manufacturing processes, producing white, green, yellow, red, blue-green, and black teas. This Chinese classification is based on the color of the wet processed leaves after infusion, with the exception of white tea, which takes on a gray-green tinge rather than white but which, when dry, has white tips.

Composition of a fresh tea leaf
(see table on page 86)

A fresh tea leaf contains more than 90 percent water, the remaining 10 percent being composed of substances present in all living tissue (protids, glucids, lipids, mineral salts) and substances found in plants (chlorophyll, cellulose, lignin, and so on). What is distinctive about tea leaves is their very high level of polyphenols, as not all plants contain such quantities. The level in tea is comparable to that found in the skin of black grapes and hence in red wine. Another characteristic of tea is that it contains alkaloids, in particular theine (caffeine), which is particularly present in the young shoots and buds. The terms theine and caffeine in fact describe the same molecule. It was isolated by two different researchers and so received two different names: in 1819 by Friedlieb Runge, a German chemist, who identified it in coffee, and in 1827 by Henry Oudry, who identified it in tea. Tea leaves start out rich in vitamin C, but as the vitamin is very sensitive to heat, it is destroyed during the manufacturing process. Tea is also rich in fluorine, which is found intact in the dry leaf.

The oxidation process

With the exception of black teas, all five other tea colors are dependent on the oxidation process and the degree to which this occurs. The oxidation of the compounds in tea leaves – notably its pigments and tannins, which turn from green or transparent to brown – happens naturally when, under the action of the molecules contained in the leaf, known as enzymes, the leaf dies: the process is one of enzymatic oxidation. All plants contain these oxidant enzymes, which are responsible for the yellowing of the leaves on trees in the fall. During the oxidation of tea leaves, the change in color, which is very visible, is the result of the polymerization of flavanols, which turn into large molecules – theaflavins and thearubigins – and give the dry leaves their tawny or gray color. Of course, the oxidation process includes a host of other invisible chemical reactions that also play their part in producing the taste of tea.

During production the oxidation process is controlled, accelerated, and sometimes halted by the grower.

DEFINITIONS

☞ FIXATION: the leaves are exposed to high temperatures to destroy the enzymes they contain that are responsible for the oxidation process.

☞ WITHERING: a process of partial dehydration aimed at making the leaves more pliable and hence easier to roll without damage (the water content is lowered from more than 90 percent to between 20 percent and 50 percent).

☞ OXIDATION: see "The oxidation process."

☞ DRYING: the leaves are dried in an oven at between 212°F and 266°F (100°C and 130°C) in order to preserve them. Between 2 percent and 4 percent of the residual humidity is retained, as many aromatic compounds are hydrophilic. This can be seen if a tea is kept too long: as it dries out, it loses its flavor.

☞ AROMA PRECURSOR: a natural, nonvolatile, nonodorous constituent of tea leaves capable of breaking down chemically or biologically into odorous molecules. These may include amino acids, glucids, organic acids, and lipids.

The role of tea processing

All the work carried out at the tea plantation, from pruning to plucking, plays its part in developing the aromatic potential of the tea. Once the tea has been harvested, it must quickly be transported to the processing plant so that the leaves do not spoil and their transformation can be controlled. Fresh tea leaves are very bitter but very rich in volatile, odorous substances and in aroma precursors. The role of the tea-processing plant, whatever color of tea is to be produced, is to promote the full development of these odorous substances and aroma precursors, and to reduce bitterness.

Whether the process involves high-heat fixation to prevent oxidation (as in the case of green and yellow teas), varying levels of chemical oxidation (for white, blue-green, and red teas) or organic fermentation (for black teas), all these processes play a complex role in bringing out the aromas of the tea. Compounds interact, polymerize, and divide to produce an aromatic bouquet and reduce the original bitterness of the fresh tea leaf.

OPPOSITE:
The colors of tea: wet leaves known as infusions laid out on the lids of tea-tasting sets.

PRECEDING PAGE:
Camellia sinensis: a "sinensis" variety from the collection of the tea importers Dammann Frères, Orgeval.

White tea

Naturally oxidized
1) Withering: 2 to 3 days
2) Drying: 10 minutes

WHITE TEA: A TEA THAT REQUIRES LITTLE PROCESSING

It seems likely that white tea was the first tea to be drunk, as processing requires a minimum of human intervention: the tea more or less processes itself, under the watchful eye of the grower. To produce the finest-quality white teas, only the buds are picked, in spring, over a very short period of two weeks when the weather is most favorable. Once picked, the tea is spread out on large bamboo racks in the shade and left like this for two or three days. This allows the tea to wither and a slow, natural enzymatic oxidation to take place, giving a gray-green color to the tea. The grower keeps a careful watch over the progress of this operation, which is extremely delicate: too much humidity in the air will cause the buds to rot; not enough humidity will make them dry out too quickly. This stage of the process is halted by drying. White tea is therefore one of the least processed and most tricky teas to produce because of its vulnerability to weather conditions.

The finest white teas come from Fujian province in China. The rarity of white tea is therefore determined by the short harvesting period each year and by the fineness of the plucking. The very finest white tea is *Bai Hao Yin Zhen* (White-Tipped Silver Needle). Only the buds are picked in spring. Other qualities are produced that contain leaves and buds, the most well known of which is *Bai Mu Dan* (White Peony). One hundred grams of *Bai Hao Yin Zhen* costs about $35 (£20), compared with $7 (£4) for the same quantity of *Bai Mu Dan*.

OPPOSITE:
Bai Hao Yin Zhen
(White-Tipped Silver Needle), Chinese white tea.

ABOVE:
Bai Mu Dan *(White Peony), Chinese white tea.*

Green tea	
Unoxidized tea	
1) Fixed at high temperature, dry or humid: 15 minutes	2) Rolling: 20 minutes to 1 hour
	3) Drying: 20 minutes

GREEN TEA: AN UNOXIDIZED TEA

Two main countries are traditionally known as producers of quality green tea: China and Japan. Green tea is not oxidized. It undergoes an initial fixation stage, which can take place in two different ways.

☞ With dry heat: the leaves are heated in a large wok over a flame or placed in a revolving cylinder into which hot air is blown – these are the two traditional Chinese methods. The shoots then take on a green-yellow color and develop dominant cooked-vegetable notes when infused.

☞ With wet heat: the leaves are placed in large bamboo baskets suspended above steam baths – this is the traditional Japanese method (formerly used in China). This method does not alter the pigment of the leaves, which retain their grass-green color, and develop dominant marine and green-plant notes.

The next stage is the rolling, which gives the tea its final shape and color. In both China and Japan, the visual qualities of tea are as important as its aroma.

☞ In China, hand rolling is still the preferred method for the finest qualities of green tea, as this allows the delicate bud on the young shoot to be protected by the leaves. The shoots can be rolled into pearls or twists, be formed into flattened sticks or needles, or be knotted together to form flowers, shells, fruit, or other shapes.

☞ In Japan, the leaf is formed into the shape of a pine needle with a dark, green glossy appearance. The stages leading to this result are many and various – rolling, pressing, kneading. The shoot is therefore no longer whole, unlike Chinese green tea, though this in no way affects its quality. In the case of *maccha*, the leaves are fixed, then dried just as they are – this is known as *tencha* – before being ground into powder in a marble mortar.

These teas are delicate and quickly lose their aroma. Ideally they should be consumed within the eight months following harvesting. Their price varies according to quality, ranging from $2.50 (£1.50) per 3 1/2 ounces (100 grams) for the poorest-quality teas to over $173 (£100) for the finest-quality spring teas.

OPPOSITE:
Sencha, *Japanese green tea.*

ABOVE:
Jade Pearl with Jasmine, *Chinese green tea.*

ABOVE:
Tencha *leaves are ground using a traditional grindstone to produce* maccha *powder.*

OPPOSITE:
Formed teas; new forms are introduced each year; as the leaves are infused and unfold, they release their hidden treasure: they often contain flower sprigs or seeds evocative of pearls.

Find the odd one out ...

The rose-colored leaves in the center of the bottom row are not tea but a plant that is drunk as an infusion like tea in China and Vietnam.

Yellow tea

Lightly fermented	
1) Fixed at high, humid temperature under cover: 15 minutes	3) Rolling: 20 minutes
2) Left standing under cover (light fermentation): 1 day	4) Drying: 20 minutes

YELLOW TEA: A LIGHTLY FERMENTED, ISLAND-GROWN TEA

The processing of yellow tea begins in the same way as Chinese green tea, except that the fixing of the leaves takes place under a covering of straw. This is followed by an extended "resting" period under cover during which some slight fermentation occurs. The tea is then delicately rolled into needles and dried. This process gives the leaf a green-yellow color and produces a golden-yellow liquor characterized by aromas with a dominant fruity, flowery note.

This tea is produced in only one place, on Jun Shan island (Jun Mountain) in Dongting Lake, Hunan province, China. The most prized of all is *Jun Shan Yin Zhen* (Jun Mountain Silver Needle), which consists only of buds. Its rarity and fineness mean that this quality of yellow tea sells for around $69 (£40) per 3 1/2 ounces (100 grams).

OPPOSITE:
Jun Shan Yin Zhen (*Jun Mountain Silver Needle*), *Chinese yellow tea.*

Red tea

Oxidized	
1) Withering: a few hours	3) Oxidation: 1 to 2 hours
2) Rolling: 20 minutes	4) Drying: 30 minutes

RED TEA: AN OXIDIZED TEA

Although known in the West as black tea because of the dark-brown color of its dried leaves, the Chinese call this red tea as, once wet, the leaves take on a tawny color. It is one of the world's most widely produced tea types.

Unlike green tea, the aim is to produce leaves that are fully oxidized. This affects the taste of the tea, which usually has a more developed structure and less bitterness as a result of the polymerization of the polyphenols, as well as "heavier" core and background aromas (see Chapter III, "Tea Tasting").

Two initial stages are required to activate the oxidation process: withering and rolling. In the withering process, the tea is spread out on large mesh-bottomed trays placed in a ventilated room for a few hours. The leaves are heated to accelerate water evaporation. When they have lost more than 50 percent of their humidity, they are sufficiently pliable for rolling. This process is carried out using a roller, a piece of equipment with two disks that turn in opposite directions. The leaf cells are broken, freeing up the enzymes and stimulating a uniform, enzymatic oxidation to take place over the entire surface of the leaf. The leaves are kneaded with varying pressure, depending on the force exerted between the disks. With Darjeeling spring teas, rolling is very light and very short, whereas with Darjeeling monsoon teas, which have tougher leaves, more pressure is used and for a longer time.

The tea is then ready for oxidation (often known as fermentation), which brings out its particular aromatic qualities. The grower's skill is knowing when to halt the oxidation: if insufficiently oxidized, the tea will be bitter with unpleasant green notes; if over oxidized, it will be flat. The shoots are arranged in layers a few centimeters thick on large white ceramic tables in a room at around 68°F (20°C). They oxidize on contact with the air. The leaves then take on a brown-red or golden-green color and the buds a beautiful golden or silvery sheen, depending on their origin. The tea is then dried in an oven at approximately 248°F (120°C). This stage is followed by the grading (separation of grades): the tea is passed through vibrating sieves to separate the broken leaves from the whole leaves. In China this tea is made into compressed cakes, which are much used among the nomadic peoples of Central Asia. The tea is molded before drying (see *Black tea*, page 105).

OPPOSITE:
Yunnan, Chinese red tea.

ABOVE:
Darjeeling, Indian red tea, North Tukvar garden, spring harvest.

FOLLOWING PAGE, LEFT:
1. Processing red tea.

2. Withering freshly harvested shoots. After rolling the tea shoots, oxidation takes place.

3. Final drying.

FOLLOWING PAGE, RIGHT:
The plantation's tea taster checks the quality of the processed teas before sending samples to tea merchants.

Blue-green or Oolong tea

Semi-oxidized

1) Withering: 1 hour

2) Semi-oxidation/rolling: 2 hours maximum

3) Drying: 20 minutes

4) Roasting: optional; time varies according to desired effect

BLUE-GREEN OR OOLONG ("BLACK DRAGON") TEA: A SEMI-OXIDIZED TEA

This tea family is halfway between a green tea and a red tea. As the degree of oxidation of the leaf is the determining factor, teas with very different aromas are produced. This is one of the most varied families and one of the richest in aromatic diversity.

The teas are known as Oolong (*wu long*) or blue-green (*qin cha*). The latter term is used mainly by producers and traders within the industry.

THE ORIGIN OF *WU LONG*

The literal meaning of *wu long* is "black dragon." According to legend, one day a tea grower was walking in his garden in Fujian, trying to find new flavors. He was deep in thought when he saw an enormous black snake emerge from a tea plant. Convinced this was an omen, he picked some leaves from the bush to sample them and that was how *wu long* tea was created.

The first stage of processing is withering, as with red tea. The young, freshly picked shoots are spread out in the sun on bamboo mats for about an hour.

The second stage combines two of the stages used in red-tea manufacturing: rolling/heating and oxidation, which are carried out alternately until the desired level of semi-oxidation is achieved.

This phase takes place in a room shaded from the light and in a warm atmosphere in order to accelerate the oxidation process. It is at this stage that the leaves are shaped – into pearls, twists, and so on. The duration of this stage depends on the type of *wu long* required.

Four major families are produced according to the degree of semi-oxidation: semi-oxidized *wu long* teas at between 5–15 percent (5–15 percent of the surface of the leaf is oxidized); 20–30 percent; 30–40 percent; and 60–70 percent.

Many *wu long* teas are then roasted to bring out the aromas of the leaf and to develop pyrogenic, toasted notes. This tradition is mainly popular among the Chinese.

The finest Oolong teas come from mainland China (Fujian and Guangdong provinces) and from Taiwan, which has specialized in and perfected the production of this type of tea.

OPPOSITE:
Anxi Tie Guan Yin,
*Chinese blue-green
(or Oolong) tea.*

ABOVE:
Bao Zhong *Taiwanese
blue-green tea.*

Black tea	
Postfermented	
1) Steam fixation	
2) Rolling/postfermentation under cover	4) Maturing in caves or cellars: from a few days to hundreds of years
3) Compressing: optional	5) Final drying to halt maturation

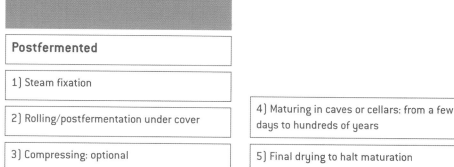

BLACK TEA: A POSTFERMENTED TEA FOR LAYING DOWN

In the West this is known as dark tea, as the dry leaves are dark without actually being black. However, once wet, the leaves turn black, which is why the Chinese call it black tea. It is the only tea family that improves with age, and it is also the only tea to undergo a genuine fermentation process comparable to the fermentation of wine.

As with green tea, after picking, the tea shoots are exposed to high heat in large pans to halt any enzymatic oxidation. The shoots are then rolled into twists while still warm to break down the cells and enable a uniform fermentation to occur. After that, they are dried until they contain no more than 10 percent residual humidity, then stored in a room at a minimum temperature of 77°F (25°C), moistened, and covered with a damp cloth topped with straw. Fermentation subsequently begins through the action of micro-organisms: this is an organic fermentation process. This stage is very important, as this is when the bouquet of the tea develops. It lasts a few days and is what some studies of tea refer to as the late fermentation of black teas. The tea is then dried. Drying varies according to intended use, as this is the maturing period.

There are two major subfamilies of black tea.
☞ Loose-leaf black teas, which either undergo accelerated drying in ovens at 158°F (70°C) for several hours and will not be suitable for ageing, or are stored in rooms to dry naturally for periods ranging from a few days to several months – the maturing process. The latter will be suitable for ageing for one or two years.
☞ Compressed black teas, which are dried over a much longer period of time, and also have a longer maturing period, which takes place in caves or cellars and lasting for up to a century! Once fermented, the shoots are placed in different-sized molds, moistened, and stored in caves or cellars with high humidity. This storage period allows the tea to develop blended aromas and to become rounder and smoother. The tea is eventually dried to halt the ageing process and to stabilize it.

The finest-quality black teas are produced in China, in five provinces: Yunnan (which produces the famous *Pu-erh* tea, which was honored with the name *gong cha*[5] under the Ming dynasty), Hubei, Hunan, Guangxi, and Sichuan. Century-old tea cakes can be worth a fortune.

OPPOSITE:
Loose-leaf Pu-erh, *Chinese black tea.*

ABOVE:
Compressed cake of Pu-erh, *Chinese black tea.*

[5] Gong cha *was the title given to the elite teas consumed by the emperor.*

THE BENEFICIAL PROPERTIES OF TEA

Tea has formed part of the traditional pharmacopoeia of Chinese medicine for more than 2,000 years. In the West, after wavering for centuries between being considered a poison or a medicament, like so many other plants from distant countries, tea is once more hitting the headlines as a plant with indisputable medicinal properties.

THE AGE-OLD EMPIRICAL VIRTUES OF TEA

In a work devoted to the legendary Shen Nong, *Shen Nong's Canon of Herbs*, written under the Han dynasty (206 BCE to 221 CE), it states that "*if one consumes tea for long enough, the body gains in strength and the mind in keenness.*"[6] Huizhong also addresses the benefits of tea, as "*lightness and clarity of mind, a detachment from worldly concerns, serenity, and liberty.*"[7]

When one reads ancient Chinese texts, the benefits attributed to tea are extremely varied.

☞ It stimulates circulation of the blood in all parts of the body.

☞ It stimulates clear thinking and a lively mind.

☞ It speeds up the elimination of alcohol in the organs of the body.

☞ It increases the body's power to resist many illnesses.

☞ It accelerates the metabolism and oxygenation of the organs of the body.

☞ It prevents tooth decay.

☞ It has a purifying and fortifying effect on the skin, helping it to remain younger-looking.

☞ It prevents or reduces anemia.

☞ It purifies urine and aids diuresis.

☞ It improves the eyes and makes them shine.

☞ It combats the effects of heat in summer (tea is by nature cold, that is, yin).

☞ It aids digestion.

☞ It eases pains in the limbs and joints.

☞ It reduces harmful mucus secretions.

☞ It eases thirst.

☞ It drives away fatigue and depression, bringing a general sense of well-being.

☞ Finally, it prolongs life.

Some of this empirical information has been confirmed by present-day scientific discoveries.

MODERN SCIENTIFIC DISCOVERIES: THE EFFECTS OF TEA

Antioxidant properties

An antioxidant molecule has the power to neutralize the free radicals that are formed in our organism as a result of internal dysfunctions or external agents such as sunlight, alcohol, and tars. These free radicals, which are responsible for damaging cell, lipid, and protein DNA, can lead to:
☞ certain types of cancer (where the DNA is affected)
☞ cardiovascular diseases (oxidation of lipids and proteins leading to the formation of low-density lipoprotein (LDL) or bad cholesterol
☞ premature ageing of tissue (oxidation of cell proteins leading to a loss of elasticity in the skin tissue particularly, and to the development of cataracts and so on).

Our organism has ways of fighting against the appearance of free radicals but a diet rich in antioxidants helps to increase their efficiency. The best-known dietary antioxidants are vitamins C and E, the carotenoids, and the flavonoids. Fruit and vegetables are recognized sources of antioxidants such as vitamins C and E and betacarotene, but there are also less well-known sources of flavonoids. A few years ago it was discovered that two plants in particular are rich in flavonoids: the tea plant and the vine.

The principal antioxidants in tea are flavanols – in particular EGCG and catechin, present mainly in green tea, and theaflavin, present in oxidized tea (red tea) – as well as derivatives of quercetin. As these molecules are soluble in water, they pass into tea liquor.

Tea is also a plant naturally rich in vitamin C (250 mg/3$\frac{1}{2}$ oz (100 g) of dry tea). However, as this is very fragile, it is completely destroyed when infused at over 86°F (30°C).

ABOVE, FROM LEFT TO RIGHT:
Inhaling the fresh, plant notes of gyokuro *Japanese green tea liquor.*

Bowl of Vietnamese green tea with lemon leaves.

[6] *From* Le Cha jing ou Classique du thé *(Cha Jing, The Classic of Tea), by Lu Yu, translated by Véronique Chevaleyre, published by Jean-Claude Gawsewitch, 2004.*

[7] *From* L'Extase du thé *(The Ecstasy of Tea), translated by Cheng Wing fun and Hervé Collet, published by Moundarren, 2002.*

Five to seven cups of tea a day (in other words, about 1 pint/$^{1}/_{2}$ liter) appears to have a noticeable effect within a few months in lowering bad cholesterol levels. Furthermore, studies carried out on animals have shown that the consumption of tea acts as a preventative against the development of tumorous cells. Research on humans is currently under way.

Tea and cosmetics

Use in antiageing creams
The antioxidant properties of tea help to slow down cell ageing, particularly in the skin. As a result, many cosmetic brands use tea extract in their antiwrinkle creams and in their aromatherapy product ranges.

Tea used for its astringent and cleansing properties
Polyphenols also have astringent and cleansing properties. Strong tea infusions can be used externally in bath water to tighten the pores of the skin and to relax; in the final rinse when washing hair to make it shine; and as a compress on the eyes to reduce puffiness. Cosmetic firms also use tea in foundation creams to reduce redness and in skin-care creams and lotions to cleanse and soothe the skin.

TEA TREE
Tea tree, *Melaleuca alternifolia*, another plant that has nothing to do with tea, is also used in cosmetics. The English name is historically derived from Captain Cook, who decided to try infusing the leaves in the same way as tea. This plant belongs to the Myrtaceae family. Native to Australia, it has been used for centuries by aborigines for its powerful antiseptic properties.

Tea and the prevention of tooth decay

Tea is also rich in fluorine. Combined with polyphenols, tea helps to strengthen tooth enamel and fight tooth decay. The action of the fluorine is enhanced by that of the polyphenols, which prevent bacteria from adhering to tooth enamel. It is also these polyphenols, found particularly in oxidized teas, that are responsible for staining tooth enamel, but this is a secondary and reversible effect. Some brands of toothpaste add green-tea extract to help reduce the buildup of dental plaque.

Tea, a gentle stimulant that relaxes and revives

It is often said that tea is a stimulant, unlike coffee, which is an excitant. Although theine and caffeine are the same molecule, the action of the molecule varies according to the medium in which it is imbibed – tea or coffee. It is a question of quantity: a cup of tea contains less theine than a cup of coffee: 20–70 mg/6 fl oz (170 ml) of tea compared with 40–115 mg/6 fl oz (170 ml) of coffee.

It is also a matter of bioavailability: in coffee, theine is in a completely free state and therefore passes very quickly into the blood, whereas in tea it forms complexes with polyphenols, part of which are not digested, the other part passing into the blood slowly. Theine is therefore liberated little by little into the blood when one drinks tea. This is even more marked if the tea is infused for a long period. In this case polyphenols pass gradually into the liquor and much more slowly than the theine, which is highly soluble in water. This is why one is recommended to discard the first lot of water in order to remove the theine from the tea (just tens of seconds are enough to eliminate 60 percent of the theine); in addition, the longer the tea infuses, the less of an excitant it becomes.

The stimulant action of tea therefore lasts over a longer period than that of coffee. It is not by chance that it became the drink of choice for Buddhist monks when meditating, its action being that of a gentle stimulant. In fact, by stimulating the central nervous system, it helps to maintain alertness but without causing edginess.

Added to this is the fact that tea is a hot drink. We know that hot drinks stimulate while relaxing us by causing the blood vessels in the skin to dilate. This reaction in the skin, which occurs a few minutes after the tea has been absorbed, can increase the sensation of warmth in cold weather and, conversely, produce a sense of coolness in hot weather by promoting heat loss.

These actions are further enhanced by that of an amino acid that is found only in tea: theanine. This induces a sense of relaxation in the brain (measured by ECG readouts showing a state between waking and sleeping).

The effects of tea on the assimilation of iron

It is often said that tea prevents the successful absorption of iron, and for this reason pregnant women are advised against drinking it. During digestion certain polyphenols do in fact remain undigested by the organism and form complexes with iron ions (that is to say, they absorb them). As a result the iron available to pass into the blood during digestion is heavily reduced. However, once it has passed into the blood there is no further interaction with the polyphenols, which are digested and also pass into the blood. It is therefore simply a matter of consuming sources of iron separately from drinking tea or of waiting some time after meals before drinking tea.

CHEMICAL FORMULA OF THEINE
(CAFFEINE)
Also known as $C_8H_{10}N_4O_2$ or 1,3,7-trimethylxanthine or 3,7-Dihydro-1,3,7-trimethyl-1H-purine-2,6-dione. It is an alkaloid of the methylxanthine family, also containing theophylline and theobromine. If one obtains an extract from the leaves and purifies it, a white powder with a bitter taste is produced.

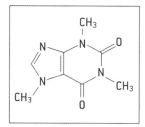

III TEA TASTING

TEA HAS RE-ESTABLISHED ITS POSITION AS A DRINK OF CONNOISSEURS. PREPARED CORRECTLY IT BECOMES A TRULY GASTRONOMIC DRINK THAT APPEALS TO ALL THE SENSES.

TEA IS ALSO A PRODUCT IMBUED WITH A STRONG CULTURAL DIMENSION. ALTHOUGH THE TEAPOT IS CENTRAL TO TEA DRINKING IN THE WEST, THIS IS NOT THE CASE IN OTHER PARTS OF THE WORLD. IN CHINA AND JAPAN, TEA DRINKING HAS DEVELOPED INTO A VERITABLE ART WITH A RANGE OF SMALL "TEA OBJECTS" BEING USED TO REVEAL AND ENHANCE THE TASTING OF THE GREAT CLASSIC TEAS.

REVEALING THE AROMATIC BOUQUET

THE FIVE GOLDEN RULES FOR PREPARING TEA IN A LARGE TEAPOT IN THE WESTERN STYLE

Water quality

Water is the medium that allows tea to express its potential; half the success of a good cup of tea depends on the water; therefore water quality is fundamental.

☞ It is important to use freshly drawn water that is pH-neutral, not too hard, even slightly acid, and very low in minerals (on a bottle of mineral water, the dry-residue rating should be as low as possible). Water filtered through an active carbon filter is a good compromise if tap water is hard and smells of chlorine.

☞ A special vessel should be used for heating the water, as water easily absorbs kitchen odors. A kettle is ideal and this should be emptied after every use (ensuring that preboiled, stale water is not reused).

Handy hint: if your water is hard and tastes of chlorine, you can leave it to stand in a pitcher overnight before pouring it into the kettle; the chalk will be deposited at the bottom of the pitcher and the smell of chlorine will have evaporated.

LU YU ON THE SUBJECT OF THE WATER FOR TEA
"Water from the mountains is the best, then river water, and finally well water … Water from slow-running streams, lakes with stony beds, or milk-white springs is the best mountain water."[1]

Lu Yu also recommended using a filter made from a copper frame with a bamboo grille covered in silk fabric:

"The commonly used filters consist of raw copper frames. The use of raw copper guarantees the freshness of the water … If you use worked copper, it will smell of the tool, and the iron will give it a foul taste."[2]

Water temperature

The temperature of the water is very important. Whatever the type of tea, the water used should never be above 203°F (95°C) as it will spoil the tea leaves; nor should the water be allowed to continue boiling for any length of time as this will cause it to lose the diluted oxygen that improves the infusion process.

The ideal water temperature varies according to the type of tea. White and green teas are at their best when made with water below 158°F (70°C). If exposed to heat higher than this, the leaves are burned, the aromas spoiled and the tea will taste very bitter. For the other tea colors, the water should be around 203°F (95°C). If the water is not sufficiently hot, it will produce a flat liquor, preventing the leaves from unfurling properly and, as a result, from releasing their full flavor.

Handy hint: if the water should be below 203°F (95°C), you can add cold water to the water from the kettle – two-thirds boiling water to one-third cold water gives water at approximately 158°F (70°C).

LU YU ON THE THREE STAGES OF BOILING

When bubbles like fish eyes form on the surface (the water) produces a scarcely audible sound, this is the first stage of boiling ... When (the water) sings around the edges like a spring and looks like an endless string of pearls, this is the second stage of boiling. When it leaps majestically like breakers on a beach and resounds like a swelling wave, this is the third stage of boiling. If boiling continues beyond this point, the water becomes unsuitable for consumption.[3]

ABOVE, FROM LEFT TO RIGHT:
Chinese bamboo strainers used in cooking but also to strain tea leaves.

Stainless-steel tea strainers, Thés de Chine, Paris.

Water at simmering point ready to be poured on to tea.

[1] *From* Le Classique du thé *(The Classic of Tea), by Lu Yu, translated by Sister Jean-Marie Vianney, published by Morel, 1977.*

[2] *From* Le Classique du thé, *by Lu Yu, ibid.*

[3] *From* Le Classique du thé, *by Lu Yu, ibid.*

Handy hint: in order to take full advantage of the fineness of Yixing clay, an initial infusion should be made to begin the seasoning process and remove the taste of the clay. To do this, you should leave a good helping of loose-leaf tea to infuse in it overnight, choosing the tea carefully according to the type of tea you want to make in the teapot. This infusion is then discarded, and you can begin using the pot to make tea. Always rinse the pot with plain water, using no soap or detergent.

Teapots in nonporous materials

If your teapot is made from nonporous material, you can still choose to season it and always use it with the same type of tea. To do this, after each infusion give the pot a quick rinse with warm water (but without rubbing away the layer of tannins that have been deposited) and leave it to dry with the lid off. Or, if you want to use it for different types of tea, after each use clean it carefully with warm water but no detergent, then wipe the inside with a clean cloth to remove the layer of tannins.

JAPANESE IRON TEAPOTS

Iron teapots form part of traditional Japanese art. Originally these were kettles and were not enameled; they went rusty, which enriched the water with iron. As well as being beautiful, iron teapots keep the tea hot and are extremely hard-wearing. However, they do require care and attention to keep them in good condition.

☞ Before using a new pot for tea, boil two or three changes of water in it to remove the metallic odor.

☞ Rinse it out with plain water after each use.

☞ Carefully dry the pot after each use to prevent the unenameled exterior from becoming rusty.

The container: the teapot

Depending on the type of tea and the country, tea may be infused in a teapot and then poured into a bowl, a glass, or a cup, or else both infused in and drunk directly from a bowl or glass.

When using a teapot, the inside should be rinsed and heated with boiling water, which should be swirled around for a few seconds before being discarded.

There are two classes of teapot: those made of porous materials such as clay and those made of nonporous materials such as glazed earthenware, porcelain, metal (cast iron, pewter, silver, and so on), or glass.

Teapots in clay, a porous material

Each time a clay teapot is used, it absorbs the aroma of the tea. It therefore needs to be seasoned and set aside for use with a particular type of tea. The tea must be full-bodied, as the teapot will absorb some of the aroma while also giving roundness to, and enriching, the liquor. This type of teapot is ideal for most red and black teas, and for many Oolong teas. To ensure that successive brews are enhanced by these embedded flavors, the teapot must be made from good-quality clay. The sides should be uniform and of a very fine grain so that the tea can "breathe" during infusion and the pot become evenly seasoned. A genuine Yixing clay teapot is ideal.

OPPOSITE:
*Small pewter Chinese
teapot with frog motif,
from Mademoiselle Li's
tea-salon collection.*

BELOW:
*Yixing painted
earthenware teapot with
dragon motif, from
Mademoiselle Li's tea-
salon collection.*

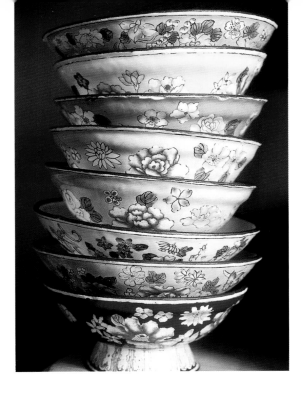

Tea quantity

The quantity of tea should be based on weight rather than volume: $1/2$ ounce for every $3^1/2$ fluid ounces (2 grams for every 10 centiliters) of water. The larger the volume of the infusion, the smaller the relative quantity of tea should be. Thus, to prepare 17 fluid ounces (50 centiliters) of tea, you need only use 3 ounces (8 grams) of tea leaves, instead of $3^1/2$ ounces (10 grams).

Handy hint: as it is not always possible to weigh the tea, for teas with leaves of average volume (most noncompressed red and black teas), allow one level teaspoonful per $3^1/2$-fluid-ounce (10-centiliter) cup (the capacity of a standard teacup). For bulkier teas (white teas, many Chinese green teas, Oolong teas), allow one good pinch of tea (using the thumb, index finger, and middle finger) per cup. For Japanese green teas, which are very dense, allow one level teaspoonful per two cups.

Length of infusion

This stage is crucial to making good tea. For example, a red spring Darjeeling left to stand for too long becomes undrinkable, whereas infused for the correct amount of time it is bright and subtle. Infusion time can vary from one to six minutes depending on the tea color, origin and harvesting period. The following table provides a guide for the main tea types.

	WATER TEMPERATURE	INFUSION TIME	WITH MILK
White tea	70°C	5–8 minutes	No
Green tea	40–90°C	1–5 minutes	No
Chinese green, spring tea	70°C	4–5 minutes	No
Other Chinese green tea	80°C	3–4 minutes	No
Japanese green, spring tea	40–60°C	1–3 minutes	No
Other Japanese green tea	80–90°C	1–3 minutes	No
Yellow tea	70°C	4–6 minutes	No
Red tea	95°C	2–5 minutes	Variable
Chinese red tea	95°C	4–5 minutes	Yes
Indian red tea – spring Darjeeling	95°C	2–3 minutes	Permitted
Indian red tea – summer or autumn Darjeeling	95°C	3–4 minutes	Yes
Indian red tea – Assam	95°C	3–4 minutes	Yes
Other red teas	95°C	4–5 minutes	Yes
Broken-leaf or ground red tea	95°C	1 minute or less according to origin, except where milk is added	Yes
Blue-green tea	95°C	5–7 minutes	No
Black tea	95°C	3–4 minutes	Permitted
Perfumed tea	95°C	According to the base tea type	Yes

Handy hint: use an electronic timer (which measures seconds as well as minutes); this will stop you forgetting the tea and allowing it to spoil.

INGREDIENTS ASSOCIATED WITH TEA

When tasting tea in order to assess its quality, nothing is added. However, certain other ingredients may be added to enhance our appreciation of tea; this may take us away from the "purist" concept of tea. In some countries, the addition of other ingredients forms an integral part of the ritual of tea making. However, for the purist, certain additions can alter the taste of the tea.

Milk

The custom of adding milk to tea appears to have been introduced by the British to reduce the bitterness of certain poor-quality imported teas, and to date from the nineteenth century. In chemical terms, the proteins in the milk form a complex with certain tannins in tea that are responsible for its pungency and bitterness, thus making the tea seem smoother and sweeter. When making tea in this way, the milk should be poured into the cup first and the hot tea added; the tea will cool on contact with the milk as it is poured. If, on the other hand, the milk is added to the hot tea, the proteins in the milk are denatured by the heat and are then unable to produce the desired smoothness. Tea tasters from some major tea companies go as far as to taste the tea with just a small drop of milk for certain blends, as they know that these are teas that will be drunk principally by tea drinkers who add milk.

Sugar

Sugar in tea is permitted, but it is preferable not to add it so that the delicate aromas of the tea are at their best. The effect of sugar is to round out all the flavors of the tea, thus producing a "simpler" liquor.

Salt

Under the Tang dynasty, salt was added to tea, and this custom persists among various Tibetan and Mongolian peoples. Salt heightens the aromas of tea and also affects the balance between sweet and bitter: salt reduces sensitivity to bitterness and therefore increases the sense of sweetness.

Citrus fruits

The addition of a slice of lemon, orange, or any other citrus fruit should be avoided as their various acidities completely change the aromas of the tea. Evidence of this is the fact that the color of the tea completely changes. However, the addition of the zest of citrus fruit, which contains essential aromatic oils free from acidity, is permitted.

Handy hint: with certain full-bodied red teas, some citrus zest may be added to the boiling water; this will give a delicate perfume to the water without destroying the aroma of the tea.

THE ART OF TEA TASTING IN CHINA AND JAPAN

China and Japan are the only two traditional, tea-consuming countries that have turned tea tasting into an art comparable with that of wine tasting in the West. Other consumer countries have codified rituals but in these the tea, often combined with other ingredients, is no longer central, thus diminishing it as a drink in its own right.

The art of tea in China

The techniques for preparing and tasting tea developed under the Ming dynasty with the expansion of tea colors. The method is known as *gong fu cha* and the utensil used is the *gaiwan* (or *zhong*).

The gong fu cha *technique*
Gong fu cha is a technique for tasting tea that involves it being served in a very careful fashion to ensure that the aromas are given full expression. It requires the use of a small Yixing clay or porcelain teapot and some small bowls. A succession of short infusions are made (between one and two minutes per change of water), using the same leaves, up to about ten infusions for fine semi-oxidized or black teas. The infusion time increases with the number of changes of water. Porcelain is preferable for lightly oxidized teas (up to 40 percent), and clay for teas that are strongly oxidized and for black teas. A large amount of tea is used, the teapot being one-third filled with tea leaves and up to half filled in the case of certain bulkier teas. This produces a true liquor with powerful, concentrated aromas, drunk from small bowls the size of *sake* bowls.

Handy hint: after using a gong fu cha *tea service, take care to drain each item thoroughly, the teapot in particular, by wedging the lid open to allow proper ventilation.*

Using the gaiwan *or* zhong
The principle of this tea-tasting method is to prepare the tea in small quantities (enough for one person) and leave the leaves to unfold fully in the water. A fine pot, usually made of porcelain, is used for Chinese white, yellow, and green teas.

Handy hint: to drink, hold the saucer, which is cooler, leaving the lid on the bowl at a slight angle to strain the tea leaves.

Preparing a gong fu cha blue-green (or Oolong) tea. Utensils needed:
1 small teapot, 1 tea boat (a shallow dish), 1 tea jar, tasting cups, optional scent cups (cylindrical, not shown), 1 tea scoop, 1 tea pick to clear tea leaves blocking the spout of the teapot, 1 pair of tongs for handling hot cups; the bamboo tray is used to dispose of excess water, as hot water must be poured over the teapot at each stage to keep it hot.
1. Fill the teapot with boiling water to rinse and warm it.
2. Empty the contents into the tea jar.
3. Use the tea jar filled with warm water to heat the outside of the teapot and the tasting cups.
4. Put tea into the teapot, pour in boiling water, cover immediately, and quickly empty into the tea jar. This stage prepares the tea leaves by heating and wetting them, but they should not be allowed to infuse. Pour the contents of the tea jar over the teapot.
5. Pour hot water onto the tea leaves, cover, and leave to infuse for about one minute.
6. Pour the liquor into the tea jar. Strain the contents of the teapot carefully into the tea jar so that the leaves do not remain steeped in the water for the next infusion.
7. If you have scent cups, pour it into these and inhale deeply. Then empty after decanting the liquor into the tasting cups (you will experience changing aromas as the scent cup cools down). Finally, drink the tea liquor from the tasting cup.

You can repeat this process several times using the same leaves and extending the infusion time by about ten seconds with every change of water.

The art of tea in Japan

The art of preparing a bowl of bitter, smooth jade-green maccha *powder*

Maccha is part of the highly codified Japanese ceremonial known as *cha no yu*. However, there is nothing to prevent you making a bowl of *maccha* for your own enjoyment or when you feel the need for a pick-me-up.

You will need a large bowl (the *chawan*), black or beige if possible, that will bring out the beautiful jade green of the *maccha* foam; a small bamboo whisk (the *chasen*); and a small scoop (the *chashaku*) for the *maccha* powder.

Unusually, you should boil the water until it reaches a full 212°F (100°C). Pour the water into the bowl and gently swirl it around to allow it to heat up the sides, then throw it away and dry the bowl carefully (no moisture should remain or lumps may form when the *maccha* is added). Put two scoops of *maccha* into the bowl. Pour boiling water on top (about 5 fluid ounces/15 centiliters: the bowl should be no more than one-third full). Break up the powder with the whisk for a few seconds, then whisk it vigorously as if writing the letter "L." To obtain a fine emulsion with the surface covered in small uniformly sized bubbles, it is important not to whisk in a circular motion.

Instead, whisk with the arm, not just the wrist, as if making an omelet. When the *maccha* is fully blended in – that is to say, when the surface is jade green with off-white glints and covered in a foam of tiny uniform bubbles – it is ready to drink.

There are no special rules about how to enjoy it. You can, as in the *cha no yu* ceremony, eat a light, dry biscuit that is low in fat, or some crystallized fruit to coat your palate in sugar, before drinking the *maccha*. In summer it can be made with very cold water to make a thirst-quenching and refreshing drink.

Maccha is a tea that spoils very quickly once it has been opened. To stop it spoiling too quickly, you can keep it in the refrigerator or even in the freezer.

The quality of the *maccha* is reflected in its color, which should be a deep, bright jade green. As it ages it turns to a yellow-green and becomes dull. A good *maccha* should be smooth and velvety with plant notes, evoking watercress or spinach, and creamy, milky notes. A poor-quality *maccha* is unbalanced, too bitter, and almost devoid of sweetness, often developing strong, fishy, marine notes.

ABOVE, FROM LEFT TO RIGHT:
Utensils for preparing a bowl of whisked maccha *from the bitter, smooth jade-powder:* maccha *is placed in the bowl, or* chawan, *using a scoop, the* chashaku; *bowl from the Palais des Thés, Paris.*

Chasen, the traditional bamboo whisk for preparing maccha; *whisk from the Chajin tea salon, Paris.*

Bowl of frothy whisked maccha.

40 GRAMS OF POWDERED TEA

Quality *maccha* tea is usually sold in 1¹/₂-ounce (40-gram) caddies. Until 20 years ago, a unit of weight known as the *monme* existed in Japan and was used for all traditional Japanese goods. Ten *monme* were equivalent to just under 1¹/₂ ounces. Tea masters knew that with this quantity they could prepare 20 bowls of light tea (*ususcha*) or 10 bowls of strong tea (*koicha*). They were therefore in the habit of ordering their tea in *monme*, and this custom has remained.

Technique for preparing a fresh liquor with plant notes

The principle is similar to that of the Chinese *gong fu cha* method, as the aim is to prepare a true tea liquor by passing several changes of water through the same tea leaves. However, unlike *gong fu cha*, the infusion time is reduced and the temperature of the water increased with each change of water. Two different preparation methods are described here: one is for *gyokuro*, a spring-harvested green tea grown in the shade; the other is for *sencha*, a green tea grown in sunlight.

TO MAKE 4 CUPS OF GYOKURO TEA

Use a small porcelain teapot – traditionally these are shaped like small casserole dishes – and small porcelain bowls the size of sake *bowls. First, warm the teapot and bowls by pouring in boiling water.*

Place 2 heaped teaspoons (approximately 5 grams) of tea in the teapot. Take 14–17 fluid ounces (40–50 centiliters) of boiling water and leave to cool to about 104°F (40°C), then pour into the teapot. Leave to stand for 3 to 4 minutes, then pour the tea liquor into the bowls. You can reuse the leaves several times by pouring on fresh water. With each change of water, the infusion time should be shortened (2 to 3 minutes, then 1 to 2 minutes, for example), the volume increased (17 fluid ounces, then 21 and 25 fluid ounces/50 centiliters, then 60 and 70 centiliters), and the temperature of the water raised (140°F, 176°F, and 190°F/60°C, then 80°C, and 90°C).

This is a tea best enjoyed on its own, or possibly accompanied by steamed fish or shellfish, with green vegetable broth or comparatively neutral-flavored pastries such as yokan.

ABOVE, FROM LEFT TO RIGHT:
Preparing gyokuro. Instead of a teapot, this traditional little terracotta dish can be used to make gyokuro; it concentrates the aromas of the tea. Place one level spoonful of tea in the dish as the capacity is very small, then pour on lukewarm water that has been left to cool in the porcelain bowl known as an uzamashi. Cover and leave to steep for 3 to 4 minutes. Serve the tea liquor with Japanese pastries. Tea service from the Chajin tea salon, Paris (except the teapot: Horaido, Kyoto).

TO MAKE 4 CUPS OF SENCHA TEA

The principle is the same as for gyokuro, but with a higher water temperature to start with (176°F/80°C, increasing to 212°F/100°C), and a much shorter infusion time (60 seconds for the first change of water, then 30 seconds, then back to 60 seconds).

USING A TEA-TASTING SET: THE INTERNATIONAL TOOL OF THE TEA EXPERT

Using a tasting set: dry leaves, infusion, and liquor

The tea-tasting set is the essential tool for tea-industry professionals in all tea-producing and -importing countries. It is always white, giving it a neutral quality, and is made of glazed earthenware or porcelain; it consists of a bowl, a cup with a perforated edge for straining the leaves, and a lid.

When a comparative tasting takes place, the tasting sets are laid out side by side. With each tea, the dry leaves are placed in a box or a small dish, and a helping of tea (usually 1/8 ounce/2 grams) is placed in the bottom of the lidded cup in which it will be infused. Once the leaves have been steeped, the lidded cup is turned over on the bowl to allow the liquor to strain into it, the leaves remaining in the cup. The wet leaves are then laid out on the upturned lid. This is known as the infusion. The liquid produced by the infusion process is known as the liquor.

The scoring system

Tea tasting should be carried out in a quiet, well-lit room, free from olfactory pollution. As with wine, it is best to spit out the tea after tasting, to avoid becoming full too quickly. A little water may be used to rinse out the mouth.

SCORING SYSTEM	OUT OF 10 POINTS
Appearance of the dry leaf	2 points
Appearance of the infusion (infused leaf)	1 point
Odor of the infusion	2 points
Color of the liquor	1 point
Flavor of the liquor (= aromas + savors)	4 points

It is important to note that the visual aspect counts for 4 points out of 10, as much as the flavor of the liquor.

Tasting set in use: Yunnan Golden Needle, Chinese red tea; Zhejiang Shi Feng Long Jing, Chinese green tea;

Fujian Anxi Tie Guan Yin, Chinese Oolong tea; Fujian Silver Needle, Chinese white tea.

THE LANGUAGE OF TEA

SIGHT: THE FIRST STAGE OF TASTING

Appeal starts with the eyes

We first begin to assess the quality of a tea with our eyes. We observe the color of the leaf when dry and wet, and also the color of the liquor, which provides much information about the tea's potential before it has even been smelled or tasted. When you visit a good tea shop, you will be invited not only to smell the tea but also to look at it to help you make your selection.

Tasting misconceptions

While the appearance of a tea can provide information about various qualitative criteria associated with it, it can also sometimes lead to presuppositions that can hamper the tasting process. For example, one often presupposes that tea with a dark liquor will be bitter, have a high theine (caffeine) content, and will be very full-bodied, whereas a tea that is pale in the cup is assumed to be low in theine and to have little aroma. However, this is rarely the case. These are tasting misconceptions.

In fact, it is mediocre, broken-leaf red teas that produce a very dark liquor, often sweetish but neither full-bodied nor high in theine (caffeine). On the other hand, a high-quality white tea steeped for ten minutes produces a very pale liquor that has body, contains a complex bouquet of aromas, and can be very high in theine (caffeine).

When describing the visual characteristics, it is usual to refer not only to the color of the leaves but also to their appearance. Are they regular in form, or, on the contrary, irregular? Are they dull or bright? The same applies to the infusion and the liquor. In the table opposite, you will find a nonexhaustive list of terms used that will help you to describe what you see.

HEARING: PRESUPPOSITIONS

Like sight, hearing can give rise to presuppositions. As a result, at professional tasting sessions no talking is allowed. Each person takes notes, and only at the end of the tasting does an exchange of opinions take place. As the senses of smell and taste are highly susceptible to influence, in order to ensure that an individual assessment regarding the quality of the tea is made, it is

COLOR CHART OF DRY AND INFUSED LEAVES		COLOR CHART OF TEA LIQUORS	
Color shades		**Color shades**	
Silvery green		Colorless	
Khaki green		Pale yellow	
Yellow green		Yellow-green	
Emerald		Lemon or mimosa yellow	
Jade		Straw yellow	
Greenish		Golden yellow	
Deep green		Pink-yellow	
Green-blue		Salmon	
Bottle green		Gray	
Green-brown		Coppery	
Russet red		Amber	
Chestnut brown		Black	
Coppery		Red-brown	
Golden		Orange-red	
Brown		Chestnut brown	
Dark		Mahogany	
Black		Ochre	
Silvery black		Caramel	
Add your own …		*Add your own …*	

Description of leaves	Description of leaves
Regular, uniform	Limpid
Bright	Opaque
Mixed	Transparent
Twists, pearls, needles, rolls, crimps, sticks …	Crystalline
	Clear
With buds	Dull
Clean	Cloudy
Brilliant (in contrast to dull, gray)	Milky
	Brilliant
Coarse, irregular (flaw)	*Add your own …*
Fibrous (negative quality)	
Stemmy (negative quality)	
Dull, gray (negative quality)	
Add your own …	

essential to taste it in silence. But there are times when hearing can have its uses …

THE SONG OF THE WATE
In the past, tea masters would listen carefully to the water being heated in order to judge the temperature it had reached. By listening to the "song" of the water, they knew when it had reached the ideal temperature for making the tea.

Water at simmering point – and in some cases just lukewarm – is poured onto the tea, which comes in a variety of colors and forms.

* *At this stage, the water is just coming to the boil.*

[4] *From L'Extase du thé (The Ecstasy of Tea), translated by Wing-fun Cheng and Hervé Collet, published by Moundarren, 2002.*

When I hear the wind in the pines and the rain in the cypresses*
I make haste to remove the remove the bronze heating pot
with its bamboo cover from the heat
Then I wait for all sound to cease
A cup of this spring snow is superior to the finest milk.

LO TAI CHING, ELEVENTH CENTURY.[4]

SMELL AND TASTE: TWO INDISSOCIABLE AND COMPLEMENTARY SENSES

When we sample tea, two senses are operating: *smell*, which captures the *aromas* when we inhale tea vapor, but also entraps them internally when we taste the tea; and *taste*, which enables us to identify the *flavors* in the mouth.

Smell: the aromatic palette of tea

When tasting tea, one begins by inhaling the smell. This activates one's *olfaction*, or sense of smell. The aromas of the tea pass through the nasal cavity and reach the sensors of the olfactory bulb, which provides a first impression of the bouquet. The perception they provide is more diffuse than that produced internally.

Then, once the tea liquor is in the mouth, *retro-olfaction* or *retronasal olfaction* (that is to say, internal olfaction) is activated by exhaling through the nose. The aromas reach the olfactory bulb by passing through the pharynx and nasal cavity. Via this route they are perceived differently from direct olfaction – on the one hand, in a more concentrated way; and on the other, they are transformed in some cases by the action of saliva and the warmth of the mouth.

To fully grasp this type of olfaction – and to isolate the sensations perceived only in the mouth – you need only pinch your nose. This gives the impression of having lost what is commonly and incorrectly called your sense of "taste" – incorrectly, as it is the perception of aromas via the retronasal route that you will in fact have lost. However, you will still perceive taste, and the thermal and tactile sensations found in the mouth.

A number of major aroma families can be identified. These families are not entirely separate; they really represent a palette with overlapping elements. Thus, a vanilla note may be sweet or leathery depending on whether one is referring to vanilla seeds or the vanilla pod. This aromatic palette refers only to the great family of "origin" teas, that is, those with their own perfume, free from added natural or synthetic aromas. And it forms the basis of a reference system.

THE TEA-AROMA FAMILIES

Animal notes
Examples: tanning, menagerie, leather, cowshed, wildcat.

Forest notes
Examples: humus, wet leaves, moss, mildew, cave, earth.

Woody notes
Examples: sandalwood, sawdust, cedar, pencil.

Coumarin-hay notes
Examples: straw, tobacco.

Sweet vanilla notes
Examples: vanilla, vanilla sugar, biscuit.

Burned notes
Examples: toast, caramel, smoked or grilled food, tar.

Spicy notes
Examples: cardamom, coriander, curry.

Floral notes
Examples: lilac, lily of the valley, freesia, rose, hyacinth, jasmine.

Fruity notes
Examples: all types of fresh, cooked, or candied fruit (except citrus fruits): red fruits, black fruits, fruits with seeds or pits (apples, pears, grapes, peaches, apricots, plums), exotic fruits.

Citrus notes
Examples: lemon, lime, bergamot.

Marine notes
Examples: seaweed, iodine, oyster.

Plant notes
Examples: green stems, cut grass, green-bean pods.

Milky notes
Examples: fresh butter, milk, cream.

ABOVE, FROM LEFT TO RIGHT:
Once you are accustomed, it is possible to tell whether or not the tea is ready from the smell of the leaves infusing in the water.

At the end of the infusion time, the tasting cups are tipped across the bowls to reveal the liquor while straining the leaves.

BELOW :
*Palette of tea-liquor colors
and aromas.*

OPPOSITE :
*Inhaling the infusion
(wetted leaves) can tell you
a lot about the different
aspects of a quality tea.*

The volatility of aromatic notes

Within the aromatic palette, not all notes have the same volatility. Therefore they don't all display the same persistence in olfaction and retro-olfaction. Some are very ephemeral, lasting only a few seconds. They can be detected only when the tea has just been steeped and is still very hot. Others are very persistent and remain in the mouth for some seconds after swallowing a mouthful of tea.

HEAD NOTES

Very volatile notes that diffuse rapidly, the effect of which fades in a few minutes.

HEART NOTES

Heavier notes that take longer to evaporate.

BACKGROUND NOTES

More persistent notes perceptible throughout the development of the odor or flavor.

In a good tea, what one looks for is a balance between these three types of notes. It can then be described as having low, medium, or high persistence in the mouth, according to the balance.

Taste: the five sensations

Although there is currently a tendency to talk more about a continuum in the field of flavor perception, five elementary taste sensations can be identified. They are: sweet, sour, bitter, salty, and *umami* (this term, which originates in Asia, has a meaning close to "flavorsome" in Japanese).

The majority of these sensations are picked up by the taste buds in the tongue, although there are also sensors in the back of the mouth, in the gums, the soft palate, and the mucous membrane of the mouth (the latter being more sensitive to tactile and thermal sensations). Temperature is very important for the perception of taste. Bitter, salty, and *umami* are less perceptible when tea is very hot; sweet, however, is accentuated by heat. On the other hand, sensitivity to sour remains unchanged by temperature variation.

These five taste sensations are odorless but they play a very important role in the way in which aromas are perceived through retro-olfaction. They serve to heighten or, conversely, to suppress aromas.

In the Chinese tradition, balance in tea is based on two qualities that must be in harmony: bitter (*ku*) and sweet (*gan*). Sweet is very different from the notion of sugary; it describes an overall impression experienced during tasting, which is a combination of a balance between taste sensations and tactile sensations. A well-balanced tea has a rather bitter attack and leaves a sweet aftertaste. An unbalanced, poor-quality, or badly made tea is too bitter or too sweet.

The vocabulary of taste sensations

Bitter
Sweet
Bittersweet
Syrupy
Sour, bright, vigorous, slightly acid
Umami
Salty
Sugary

TOUCH: THE TEXTURE OF THE LEAF AND THE LIQUOR

When tasting, touch also plays a part in assessing the quality of the tea. In fact, the freshness of the dry leaf is judged by handling it. It should be relatively pliable, and above all not brittle. If it *is* brittle, this means that the leaf has dried out too much, either because it was overdried during manufacture or because it is too old. In both cases, the tea loses much of its aromatic complexity and becomes more astringent, and therefore unbalanced.

The sensation of touch is also perceptible in the mouth. As well as the five taste sensations, there are also tactile sensations in the mouth that pick up the texture of the tea.

The vocabulary of touch sensations

Below are examples of the kind of vocabulary relating to touch used by tea tasters to describe the feel of the dry leaf and the liquor; here the infusion is less important in describing the tea.

Dry leaf
Silky, downy, dusty, rough (negative quality), brittle (negative quality: leaf that is too dry or old), supple, heavy (well rolled, tightly packed), light (negative quality: badly rolled, too open).

Liquor
Astringent, pungent, pure (concentrated as opposed to diluted, or else with a "clean" unmixed taste: no parasitical flavors), dense, thick (for example, one can say that a liquor "has thickness" or "a thick quality"), diluted, smooth, full, voluminous, flat, mellow, flavorsome, rounded, metallic, full-bodied, suave, intense, heavy, light (negative quality: lacking in body), strong, muddy, velvety, supple, fluid, solid.

FLAVOR: A COMBINATION OF SMELL, TASTE, AND TOUCH

The flavor of a tea is a complex perception obtained by combining the taste sensations perceived on the tongue (taste), the aromas perceived via the olfactory and retronasal (smell) routes, and the tactile and thermal sensations perceived in the mouth (touch). All this sensory information reaches the brain without our really being able to distinguish it, which is what makes the tasting experience so magical.

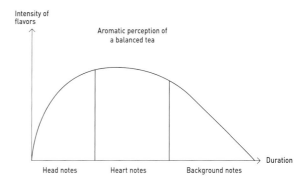

The role of taste sensations is to balance the perception of flavors by heightening their odor to a greater or lesser extent, and by altering their texture similarly.

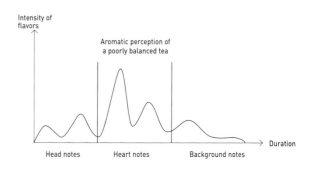

Possible defects in tea

Among the most common flaws found in tea are imbalances between sweet and bitter; burned notes; dullness; and insipidness. These can be due to a number of factors.
☞ Poor growing and harvesting conditions (for example, too much rain).
☞ Poor manufacturing process (for example, excessive withering, poorly controlled oxidation).
☞ Poor preparation (for example, poor-quality water, too hot water, wrong quantity of tea).

ABOVE :
Bai Hao Wu Long
(Oriental Beauty), Oolong
tea infusion.

OPPOSITE :
Didier Jumeau-Lafond
weighing out tea at a
tasting session, Dammann
Frères, Orgeval.

TASTING THE 32 *GRAND CRU* TEAS

THE 32 *GRAND CRU* TEAS: SPECIAL CHARACTERISTICS

Not all tea-producing countries are included here; only the most representative have been selected. With regard to tea colors, the examples given belong to the classic families within each type; more recent creations are not included. For example, production of a quality Oolong tea has been under development for some years now in Darjeeling, although historically Darjeeling is known for its red teas. Hence, reference is made here only to red teas originating in Darjeeling. Traditionally, the great Oolong producers were in mainland China, mainly in Fujian, and in Taiwan; this family is therefore represented by teas that originate in these two regions.

With the following profiles, the aim is not to provide an exhaustive available list of teas, but rather to offer a basic tool to assist in tea tasting and help both newcomers and more knowledgeable tea enthusiasts to take their first steps in tea tasting.

To ensure uniform tasting standards, the tasting technique is that employed with a professional tasting set. However, information is also given on the equipment best suited to ensuring that individual teas are able to achieve their full aromatic potential.

Bai Hao Yin Zhen
White-Tipped Silver Needle

Mainland China

Tea type: white tea, imperial harvest.
Place of production: Fujian province.

Preparation advice
Use a *gaiwan* (or *zhong*) or a glass.

Dry leaf
Appearance: silvery-green downy buds.
Odor: privet attack, dry grass, background cocoa.

Infused leaf or infusion
Appearance: jade green, uniform.
Odor: Roast chestnut, cocoa with a sorrel note.

Liquor
Color: limpid, pale yellow with hints of pink on cooling.
Odor: same nose as the infusion.
In the mouth: velvety texture, developed sweet quality, little bitterness. Chestnut head note, then a violet, flowery note.

Accompanying dishes
Mild dishes: steamed poultry, tofu, milky desserts.

Bai Mu Dan
White Peony

Mainland China

Tea type: white tea, fine harvest.
Place of production: Fujian province.

Preparation advice
Use a *gaiwan* (or *zhong*) or a glass.

Dry leaf
Appearance: silvery-green downy buds and a majority of dark-green leaves.
Odor: dry-wood attack, grilled note.

Infused leaf or infusion
Appearance: jade-green buds and tawny leaves.
Odor: fruity apricot and flowery English rose.

Liquor
Color: limpid, pale yellow.
Odor: same nose as the infusion with a cocoa note.
In the mouth: slight astringency and acidity, thick. Zesty head note, then cocoa and flowery notes.

Accompanying dishes
Dishes with gentle, honeyed notes.

Shi Feng Long Jing
Lion Peak Dragon Well

Mainland China

Tea type: pan-dried green tea shaped in flattened sticks, fine spring harvest.
Place of production: Zhejiang province.

Preparation advice
Use a *gaiwan* (or *zhong*) or a glass.

Dry leaf
Appearance: leaf flattened into sticks, the two leaves enclosing the bud, yellow-green highlights, very regular.
Odor: plant attack, with a soft vanilla, chestnut note.

Infused leaf or infusion
Appearance: jade-green leaf, shoot visible if finely picked. Two leaves and a bud.
Odor: plant and water-cooked chestnut.

Liquor
Color: limpid, pale yellow, bright.
Odor: vanilla, chestnut.
In the mouth: velvety, slightly bitter, rounded, plant, vanilla, and water-cooked chestnut notes.

Accompanying dishes
Steamed dishes.

Bi Luo Chun

Green Spring Snail

Mainland China

Tea type: pan-dried green tea shaped in twists to produce a "curled" appearance, fine spring harvest.
Place of production: Jiangsu province.

Preparation advice
Use a *gaiwan* (or *zhong*) or a glass.

Dry leaf
Appearance: fine gray-green appearance with curly silvery down.
Odor: woody and animal.

Infused leaf or infusion
Appearance: fine plucking (bud and two small, young leaves), green-yellow.
Odor: nose faithful to the dry leaf.

Liquor
Color: limpid, golden yellow.
Odor: pronounced marine note with notes of the infusion.
In the mouth: strongly bitter and velvety, marine notes, green plant and woody notes.

Accompanying dishes
Grilled poultry, dry fruit, vanilla or coconut dessert.

Gu Zhu Zi Sun

Mount Gu Zhu Purple Bamboo shoot

Mainland China

Tea type: lightly pan-dried green tea, worked while hot into the curved shape of young bamboo shoots, fine spring harvest.
Place of production: Zhejiang province.

Preparation advice
Use a *gaiwan* (or *zhong*) or a glass.

Dry leaf
Appearance: small, curved, downy green shoots.
Odor: plant and soft vanilla notes.

Infused leaf or infusion
Appearance: small, immature shoot with two leaves still enclosing a green-yellow bud.
Odor: ozone and buttery notes.

Liquor
Color: limpid, pale yellow.
Odor: chestnut and cooked green bean notes.
In the mouth : faithful to the odor with a well-balanced bittersweetness and velvetiness, good aromatic persistence.

Accompanying dishes
Pan-fried vegetables, poultry broth, vanilla dessert.

Jade Pearl with Jasmine

Mainland China

Tea type: pearl-shaped green tea, imperial autumn harvest.
Place of production: Fujian province.

Preparation advice
Use a *gaiwan* (or *zhong*).

Dry leaf
Appearance: downy silvery-green pearls. No jasmine petals.
Odor: Jasmine and soft vanilla notes.

Infused leaf or infusion
Appearance: jade-green buds.
Odor: faithful to the dry leaf with a chestnut note.

Liquor
Color: pale yellow.
Odor: green plant with a jasmine background.
In the mouth: very flowery, jasmine with a green plant background.

Accompanying dishes
Coconut milk desserts, poultry broths.

Gyokuro
Pearl Dew

Japan

Tea type: needle-shaped green tea, grown in the shade, spring harvest.
Place of production: Uji.

Preparation advice
Small porcelain teapot, drink in small porcelain cups.

Dry leaf
Appearance: small green-blue leaf with a glazed appearance.
Odor: watercress, sorrel, flowery.

Infused leaf or infusion
Appearance: pieces of dark-green shoot.
Odor: faithful to the dry leaf with a gentle marine background note.

Liquor
Color: yellow-green, pale, cloudy, milky appearance.
Odor: watercress and soft marine notes.
In the mouth: milky, plant, and soft marine notes, slight acidity, velvety.

Accompanying dishes
Seafood, sushi, Japanese desserts using bean paste or rice powder.

Sencha

Japan

Tea type: needle-shaped green tea, grown in sunlight, summer harvest.
Place of production: Shizuoka district.

Preparation advice
Small porcelain teapot, drink in small porcelain cups.

Dry leaf
Appearance: shiny jade-green needles.
Odor: green plant and iodized marine.

Infused leaf or infusion
Appearance: pieces of small, unfolded, jade-green shoot.
Odor: nose faithful to the dry leaf with a more marked iodized note.

Liquor
Color: pale yellow-green, transparent.
Odor: nose faithful to the infusion.
In the mouth: powerful marine and plant notes, robust, slight bitterness.

Accompanying dishes
Seafood, saltwater fish grilled or poached in stock.

Genmaicha
Popcorn Tea

Japan

Tea type: sencha mixed with rice and popcorn.
Place of production: Shizuoka district.

Preparation advice
Large teapot, drink in bowls or cups.

Dry leaf
Appearance: shiny jade-green needles strewn with rice grains and popcorn.
Odor: grain with marine and green plant background.

Infused leaf or infusion
Appearance: pieces of small, unfolded, jade-green shoot with rice and popcorn.
Odor: green plant, marine, and roasted grain notes.

Liquor
Color: yellow-green.
Odor: faithful to the infusion.
In the mouth: notes faithful to the odor with acidity giving robustness.

Accompanying dishes
Grilled food, brunch with bacon and eggs.

Bancha Hojicha
Roasted Bancha Leaves

Japan

Tea type: roasted green tea, mature leaves, autumn harvest.
Place of production: Shizuoka district.

Preparation advice
Large teapot, drink in bowls or cups.

Dry leaf
Appearance: chestnut "shavings."
Odor: a woody cedar note, caramelized.

Infused leaf or infusion
Appearance: unfolded green-chestnut leaves.
Odor: faithful to the nose of the dry leaf.

Liquor
Color: amber.
Odor: endive.
In the mouth: cedar woodiness, soft vanilla, no bitterness, very rounded.

Accompanying dishes
Sushi, *yakitori*, brunch, chocolate or vanilla desserts.

Jun Shan Yin Zhen
Jun Mountain Silver Needle

Mainland China

Tea type: yellow tea, imperial harvest.
Place of production: Hunan province.

Preparation advice
Use a *gaiwan* (or *zhong*).

Dry leaf
Appearance: long green-yellow buds.
Odor: burned and cocoa-bean notes.

Infused leaf or infusion
Appearance: green-yellow buds.
Odor: roast chestnut note.

Liquor
Color: pale yellow.
Odor: soft vanilla note.
In the mouth: exotic fruit and soft vanilla notes.

Accompanying dishes
Mushrooms in cream, tofu, milky desserts using coconut milk.

Wen Shan Bao Zhong[5] (ou Pouchong)
Wen Mountain Paper Packet

Taiwan

Tea type: Oolong, semi-oxidized to 8–12 percent, fine picking.
Place of production: Wen Mountain, Ping Lin village, near Taipei.

Preparation advice
Gong fu cha method, drink from small porcelain or enameled clay cups.

Dry leaf
Appearance: large dark-green leaves, lightly twisted lengthways.
Odor: woody vegetable and flowery jasmine notes.

Infused leaf or infusion
Appearance: large dark-green leaves from a fine picking of well-developed shoots.
Odor: faithful to the dry leaf.

Liquor
Color: mimosa yellow.
Odor: faithful to the infusion.
In the mouth: jasmine note and peach background, acidity giving freshness and slight bitterness.

Accompanying dishes
Dried fruits, milky desserts.

Gao Shan Cha
High-Mountain Tea (Jin Shuen)

Taiwan

Tea type: Oolong, semi-oxidized to 12–15 percent, fine picking.
Place of production: Nantou and Jayi regions.

Preparation advice
Gong fu cha method, drink from small porcelain or enameled clay cups.

Dry leaf
Appearance : dark-green leaves rolled into small pearls.
Odor: buttery and candied coconut notes.

Infused leaf or infusion
Appearance: large dark-green leaves from a fine picking of well-developed shoots.
Odor: faithful to the dry leaf.

Liquor
Color: straw yellow.
Odor: candied coconut note.
In the mouth: flowery jasmine and buttery notes with a candied coconut aftertaste, slight bitterness, acidity, velvety.

Accompanying dishes
Dried fruits, milky desserts.

Dong Ding (or Tung Ting) Oolong
Frozen-Peak Oolong

Taiwan

Tea type: Oolong, semi-oxidized to 20 percent, fine picking.
Place of production: Nantou region, Dong Ding mountain.

Preparation advice
Gong fu cha method, drink from small porcelain or enameled clay cups.

Dry leaf
Appearance : dark-green leaves rolled into small pearls.
Odor: buttery note, flowery and vegetable notes.

Infused leaf or infusion
Appearance: large dark-green leaves from a fine picking of well-developed shoots.
Odor: plant and soft vanilla notes.

Liquor
Color: straw yellow.
Odor: biscuity, vanilla, and flowery notes.
In the mouth : flowery gardenia notes, buttery and soft vanilla, light bitterness, velvety.

Accompanying dishes
Dried fruits, milky desserts.

Anxi Tie Guan Yin
Anxi Iron Goddess of Mercy

Mainland China

Tea type: Oolong, semi-oxidized to 20–25 percent, roasted, fine picking.
Place of production: Fujian province, near the town of Anxi.

Preparation advice
Gong fu cha method, drink from small porcelain or enameled clay cups.

Dry leaf
Appearance: leaves rolled into large jade-green pearls with small chestnut-brown stems.
Odor: flowery notes of hyacinth and linden, soft vanilla note.

Infused leaf or infusion
Appearance : large dark-green leaves from a fine picking of well-developed shoots.
Odor: ozone head notes and caramelized red fruit background notes.

Liquor
Color: straw yellow.
Odor: flowery hyacinth note.
In the mouth: flowery hyacinth attack, persistent white peach background note, very slight bitter flavor, no acidity, velvety and smooth.

Accompanying dishes
Dried fruits, milky desserts.

Feng Huang Dan Cong
Feng Huang Tree[6]

Mainland China

Tea type: Oolong, semi-oxidized to 20–25 percent, roasted, picking of young shoots with well-developed buds.
Place of production: Guangdong province, Feng Huang mountain.

Preparation advice
Gong fu cha method, drink from small porcelain or enameled clay cups.

Dry leaf
Appearance: long, twisted chestnut-brown shoots.
Odor: roasted, fruity notes.

Infused leaf or infusion
Appearance: long green shoots with chestnut highlights.
Odor: exotic fruits.

Liquor
Color: coppery amber.
Odor: faithful to the dry leaf.
In the mouth: exotic fruit and grilled notes with strong persistence, developing to a flowery freesia note, slight bitterness.

Accompanying dishes
Caramelized fruit tart (upside-down tart).

Wu Yi Da Hong Pao
Wu Yi Mountain Big Red Robe

Mainland China

Tea type: Oolong, semi-oxidized to 40 percent, roasted, picking of young shoots with well-developed buds.
Place of production: Fujian province, Wu Yi Mountain.

Preparation advice
Gong fu cha method, drink from small porcelain or enameled clay cups.

Dry leaf
Appearance: long, twisted green-chestnut shoots.
Odor: grilled, praline note.

Infused leaf or infusion
Appearance: long, unfolded green-chestnut leaves.
Odor: faithful to the dry leaf with a woody, waxed-wood head note and a marine seaweed background note.

Liquor
Color: dark amber.
Odor: dominant woody note.
In the mouth: faithful to the infusion with a touch of acidity and slight bitterness.

Accompanying dishes
Grilled fish, grilled tofu, praline desserts.

Bai Hao Wu Long
White-Tipped Oolong (often known as Oriental Beauty)

Taiwan

Tea type: Oolong, semi-oxidized to 60–70 percent, fine picking.
Place of production: Hsinchu and Taoyuan regions.

Preparation advice
Gong fu cha method, drink from small porcelain or enameled clay cups.

Dry leaf
Appearance: twisted chestnut shoots, slightly shriveled with silvery, downy buds.
Odor: flowery and woody.

Infused leaf or infusion
Appearance: fine chestnut shoots and buds.
Odor: flowery rose and fruity, stewed plum.

Liquor
Color: amber.
Odor: faithful to the infusion.
In the mouth: velvety with a flowery rose attack and a fruity, woody persistence, no bitterness.

Accompanying dishes
Salty-sweet *tagines*, desserts made with white chocolate or milk, dried fruits.

Dian[7] Hong Gongfu[8]
Yunnan Red Gongfu

Mainland China

Tea type: oxidized tea, fine picking.
Place of production: Yunnan province.

Preparation advice
Large teapot, drink from a bowl or cup.

Dry leaf
Appearance: large tawny shoots, twisted and downy.
Odor: woody and flowery notes.

Infused leaf or infusion
Appearance: unfolded, uniform tawny shoots.
Odor: woody and blond tobacco notes.

Liquor
Color: dark amber.
Odor: faithful to the nose of the infusion.
In the mouth: slight astringency and bitterness, full-bodied, flowery and spicy, tobacco and honey notes.

Accompanying dishes
Lamb or mutton *tagines* with dried fruits (apricots, dates, and so on), chocolate desserts, stewed autumn fruits.

Qi Men Hong Gongfu
Keemun Red Gongfu

Mainland China

Tea type: oxidized tea, fine picking.
Place of production: Anhui province, near the village of Qi Men.

Preparation advice
Large teapot, drink from a bowl or cup.

Dry leaf
Appearance: small, twisted black shoots with buds having silvery highlights.
Odor: dry wood, leather, cocoa bean notes.

Infused leaf or infusion
Appearance: small, unfolded tawny shoots.
Odor: faithful to the dry leaf with a forest background note.

Liquor
Color: deep red.
Odor: faithful to the dry leaf.
In the mouth: predominant cocoa powder note, leather note, velvety, very rounded.

Accompanying dishes
Grilled red meats, particularly duck, dark chocolate desserts.

Darjeeling North Tukvar
Grade SFTGFOP1

Northern India

Tea type: oxidized tea, fine spring picking.
Place of production: North Tukvar tea garden, Darjeeling estates.

Preparation advice
Large teapot, drink from a bowl or cup.

Dry leaf
Appearance: young green-chestnut shoots with many downy, silvery buds.
Odor: green stem and white flower notes.

Infused leaf or infusion
Appearance: small, unfolded green shoots.
Odor: faithful to the dry leaf.

Liquor
Color: straw yellow.
Odor: faithful to the infusion.
In the mouth: astringency and bitterness revealing a green plant and flowery gardenia bouquet.

Accompanying dishes
Frozen milk desserts.

Darjeeling Phuguri
Grade SFTGFOP

Northern India

Tea type: oxidized tea, fine summer picking.
Place of production: Phuguri tea garden, Darjeeling estates.

Preparation advice
Large teapot, drink from a bowl or cup.

Dry leaf
Appearance: young chestnut shoots with many downy, silvery buds.
Odor: woody and flowery.

Infused leaf or infusion
Appearance: small, unfolded green and tawny shoots.
Odor: faithful to the dry leaf with a pronounced flowery rose note and an orange zest note.

Liquor
Color: golden yellow.
Odor: faithful to the infusion.
In the mouth: slight bitterness, full-bodied, revealing a plant and flowery bouquet.

Accompanying dishes
Brunch, pear-based desserts.

Assam Maijian
Grade TGFOP

Northern India

Tea type: oxidized tea, fine summer picking.
Place of production: Maijian tea garden, Assam estates.

Preparation advice
Large teapot, drink from a bowl or cup.

Dry leaf
Appearance: long, twisted, downy, chestnut-brown shoots, strewn with many golden buds.
Odor: flowery, tobacco, spicy.

Infused leaf or infusion
Appearance: long, unfolded tawny shoots.
Odor: tobacco, stewed autumn fruits, henna.

Liquor
Color: coppery.
Odor: faithful to the infusion.
In the mouth: astringency and acidity revealing a spicy, tobacco, and stewed fruit bouquet.

Accompanying dishes
Brunch, mutton or lamb *tagines*.

Nilgiri Thiashola
Grade TGFOP

Southern India

Tea type: oxidized tea, fine picking.
Place of production: Thiashola garden, Nilgiri estates.

Preparation advice
Large teapot, drink from a bowl or cup.

Dry leaf
Appearance: fine, regular, twisted chestnut-brown shoots.
Odor: woody, stewed, spiced fruit.

Infused leaf or infusion
Appearance: tawny shoots with green highlights.
Odor: woody, henna, fruity.

Liquor
Color: pale amber.
Odor: woody and stewed plums.
In the mouth : robustness worthy of Darjeeling, fruity, flowery, and plant notes.

Accompanying dishes
Vanilla milk desserts, poached fruits.

Ceylon Lover's Leap
Grade FOP

Sri Lanka

Tea type: oxidized tea, medium picking with developed leaves.
Place of production: Lover's Leap garden, Nuwara Eliya district.

Preparation advice
Large teapot, drink from a bowl or cup.

Dry leaf
Appearance: twisted, deep chestnut-brown shoots.
Odor: flowery and woody.

Infused leaf or infusion
Appearance: long chestnut-brown shoots.
Odor: faithful to the dry leaf with a henna note.

Liquor
Color: coppery.
Odor: woody and spicy.
In the mouth: slight astringency and sourness revealing a woody, fruity, spicy note.

Accompanying dishes
Brunch, milk desserts, poultry.

Kenya Marynin
Grade FBOP

Kenya

Tea type: oxidized tea, medium picking with developed and broken leaves.
Place of production: Marynin garden.

Preparation advice
Large teapot, drink from a bowl or cup.

Dry leaf
Appearance: broken, deep chestnut-brown shoots.
Odor: woody.

Infused leaf or infusion
Appearance: broken tawny shoots.
Odor: henna, woody.

Liquor
Color: deep copper.
Odor: faithful to the infusion.
In the mouth: slight astringency and bitterness revealing a dominant woody, spicy note.

Accompanying dishes
Brunch.

Ancient Pu-erh

Mainland China

Tea type: black tea, imperial harvest.
Place of production: Yunnan province.

Preparation advice
Gong fu cha method, drink from small porcelain, stoneware, or enameled clay cups.

Dry leaf
Appearance: small pale-chestnut shoots in compressed, downy twists.
Odor: woody, cedar, moss.

Infused leaf or infusion
Appearance: small black shoots.
Odor: damp undergrowth, licorice.

Liquor
Color: dense, opaque chestnut.
Odor: faithful to the dry leaf.
In the mouth: no bitterness or astringency, velvety "thickness" revealing a bouquet of soft woody, damp moss, and licorice aromas.

Accompanying dishes
Game in sauce, caramelized desserts.

Vintage Pu-erh

Mainland China

Tea type: black tea, fine picking.
Place of production: Yunnan province.

Preparation advice
Large teapot, drink from bowls or cups.

Dry leaf
Appearance: small, twisted, downy, pale chestnut-brown shoots.
Odor: woody, earthy.

Infused leaf or infusion
Appearance: small black shoots.
Odor: faithful to the dry leaf with a leaf litter note.

Liquor
Color: deep chestnut, very dense, almost coffee-colored.
Odor: faithful to the infusion.
In the mouth: slight acidity, no bitterness or astringency, velvety and powdery revealing a forest and slightly marine bouquet.

Accompanying dishes
Red meats in sauce or grilled, caramelized desserts.

Marco Polo

Aromatized tea

Tea type: aromatized Chinese red tea with flowers and fruit from China and Tibet.

Preparation advice
Large teapot, drink from bowls or cups.

Dry leaf
Appearance: long, deep chestnut-brown shoots.
Odor: woody tea note with soft vanilla and honey notes and a touch of citrus.

Infused leaf or infusion
Appearance: tawny shoots.
Odor: woody, henna, lavender flower, and fruity bergamot.

Liquor
Color: amber.
Odor: flowery and vanilla.
In the mouth: excellent roundness, faithful to the odor with a pronounced zesty note.

Accompanying dishes
Brunch, exotic fruit tarts, honey-based pastries.

Hamman Tea

Aromatized tea

Tea type: bancha green tea mixed with red fruits, orange blossom, and rose petals.

Preparation advice
Large teapot, drink from bowls or cups.

Dry leaf
Appearance: long jade-green shoots with dried fruit pieces and flower petals.
Odor: green plant notes, red fruits, flowery.

Infused leaf or infusion
Appearance: unfolded jade-green shoots with fruit pieces and flower petals.
Odor: faithful to the dry leaf with a dominant plant note.

Liquor
Color: yellow-green.
Odor: faithful to the dry leaf.
In the mouth: slight acidity heightening the green plant note and giving a sensation of "freshness" enhanced by red fruit and flower notes.

Accompanying dishes
Fruit salads, fruits in jelly.

Goût Russe Douchka

Aromatized tea

Tea type: blend of red teas from Sri Lanka, India, and China, aromatized with citrus.

Preparation advice
Large teapot, drink from bowls or cups.

Dry leaf
Appearance: small, deep chestnut-brown shoots strewn with citrus peel.
Odor: woody with citrus peel (no flesh).

Infused leaf or infusion
Appearance: tawny tea shoots strewn with citrus peel.
Odor: faithful to the dry leaf with a dominant bergamot note among the citrus.

Liquor
Color: coppery.
Odor: faithful to the infusion.
In the mouth: rounded and full-bodied with slight bitterness and acidity, woody background note with a dominant bergamot and citrus orange note.

Accompanying dishes
Brunch, dark chocolate tart, plain cookies, sponge cakes.

Earl Grey Blue Flower

Aromatized tea

Tea type: blend of red teas from Sri Lanka, India, and China, aromatized with citrus and bergamot, and strewn with cornflower petals.

Preparation advice
Large teapot, drink from bowls or cups.

Dry leaf
Appearance: small, deep chestnut-brown shoots with cornflower petals.
Odor: woody, flowery, and bergamot.

Infused leaf or infusion
Appearance: tawny tea shoots strewn with cornflower petals.
Odor: faithful to the dry leaf with a clear, woody, red tea note.

Liquor
Color: coppery.
Odor: faithful to the dry leaf.
In the mouth: round and full-bodied, woody and bergamot notes to finish.

Accompanying dishes
Brunch, dark chocolate tart, plain cookies, sponge cakes.

[5] Bao Zhong *means "wrapped in paper": in China, tea is traditionally sold wrapped in small square paper packets.*

[6] *The name comes from the fact that, traditionally, the tea is harvested from very old, wild tea plants, each having its own particular gustatory qualities, as the teas harvested from the different tea plants are not blended. The tea shown here is not from these vintage plants, as it is very difficult to find in the European market and is very expensive. It comes instead from a harvest of high-quality tea of the same "appellation," growing at the foot of Feng Huang mountain, and economically far more accessible to the general public.*

[7] Dian *is the abbreviation of Yunnan.*

[8] *In China, Gongfu is a grade describing red tea that is picked very fine, unlike Souchong, which is harvested more coarsely, making it ideal for use in smoked teas.*

DRAWING UP YOUR AROMATIC PALETTE

You can use the table below to record your own experiences as you learn about the art of tea tasting. Under the heading "referent," you can describe the type of olfactory sensation experienced. When you smell an odor you have encountered before, you often begin by remembering a place – known only to you. Then, if you concentrate further, various other memories of smells associated with this place will come back to you. You will need to work at recapturing the original olfactory note – the one that evokes this odor encountered in the past. This original note becomes a referent comprehensible to all, or at least to all those who share a common culture. If you go to Japan, the referents will not be the same: where a Western person might identify a damp, mossy note, a Japanese person may experience fermented seaweed!

OPPOSITE:
When inhaling the fragrances of tea liquors, and exploring the recollections and associations they evoke, you will find flowery and soft vanilla aromatic notes …

Family	Place experienced	Evocations	Referent	Found in the following tea
Animal (example)	Tack room	Horse, saddle, rain	Wet leather	Current year, loose-leaf Pu-erh
Hesperidia or citrus (example)	Tea at grandmother's	Cookies, milk, tea, aromatized tea leaves	Bergamot	Earl Grey Imperial
Animal				
Forest				
Woody				
Soft vanilla				
Milky				
Pyrogenic				
Spicy				
Fruity				
Hesperidia or citrus				
Floral				
Marine				
Plant				

IV THE SUBTLE AFFINITIES OF TEA

TEA EVOKES A UNIVERSE OF TASTES AND AROMAS. IT IS A GOURMET DRINK THAT LENDS ITSELF TO THE EXPLORATION OF OTHER FINE PRODUCTS THAT ALSO APPEAL TO THE SENSES.

OUR FIRST ENCOUNTER IS WITH TWO OTHER FASCINATING PRODUCTS THAT ALSO ORIGINATE IN FAR-OFF COUNTRIES AND HAVE FOLLOWED A HISTORY SIMILAR TO THAT OF TEA: COFFEE AND CHOCOLATE. IN RECENT YEARS, WITH THE DEVELOPMENT OF THE *WORLD FOOD* MOVEMENT, TEA AND COFFEE, AND TEA AND CHOCOLATE, HAVE ENJOYED A HAPPY ASSOCIATION OF AROMAS AND FLAVORS.

THE SECOND AFFINITY WE EXPLORE IS THAT BETWEEN TEA AND WINE. WITH SO MUCH IN COMMON IN TERMS OF CULTURE AND CONSUMPTION, TEA AND WINE OFTEN COME TOGETHER TO BE ENJOYED AT MEALTIMES.

AND FINALLY, A MORE EPHEMERAL PAIRING IS THAT BETWEEN TEA AND PERFUME; HERE A PALETTE OF ODORS ARE FOUND THAT CAN PRODUCE MUTUALLY INSPIRING COMBINATIONS.

TEA, COFFEE, AND COCOA

PRODUCTS OF DISTANT SHORES

Three continents

Tea, coffee, and cocoa are plants that grow in tropical regions, originating in three different continents. Coffee originates in Africa, in southwest Ethiopia in the provinces of Kaffa and Sidamo; cocoa originates in the south of North America, in Mexico, and in the north of South America, in the depths of Amazonia; and tea originates in Asia, high up in the mountains of southwest China.

Three botanical families

These plants belong to different botanical families. Coffee, like gardenia and cinchona, is a member of the family Rubiaceae, of the genus *Coffea*. Cocoa, like the kola nut, belongs to the family Sterculiaceae, genus *Theobroma*. Tea belongs to the family Theaceae, genus *Camellia*. In the case of cocoa and coffee, it is the ripe seeds extracted from the fruit that are used; in the case of tea, it is the young leaves that are harvested.

DRINKS WITH SIMILAR HISTORIES

Drinks associated with divinity

Coffee and tea were originally consumed for their stimulating properties and were prepared as a decoction: coffee by the Sufis to accompany their prayers, and tea by Buddhist monks to accompany their meditations. According to one of the tenth-century tales of the *Thousand and One Nights*, coffee was discovered when a young Yemeni goatherd who, puzzled by the constant state of excitement exhibited by his goats, noticed that they were very fond of the red berries growing on a certain type of bush. He tried them himself and found that they made him joyful and full of energy. The Sufi monks in the community to which he brought his discovery decided to prepare a decoction of the berries and adopted the custom of drinking it during their prayers in order to stay alert. This brew became known as "wine of Arabia" as opposed to the "wine of Mass" consumed by Christians. From the earliest times, cocoa was held sacred by the Mayan people, the Toltecs, and then the Aztecs. In the tenth century, the cacao tree was

considered sacred, and venerated and cultivated by the high priest and king of the Toltec people, Quetzalcóatl, who was reincarnated in the form of a plumed serpent. The Toltecs devoted a cult to the reincarnated Quetzalcóatl and ritualized the consumption of cocoa by transforming it into a drink. In the fourteenth century this legacy was taken up by the Aztecs who used it during sacrificial ceremonies, adding a red coloring, annatto, symbolizing death.

From currency to European object of desire

Cocoa beans and cakes of tea were used as a form of currency in the regions in which they originated, and took on a not inconsiderable economic dimension. Both formed part of the tribute collected in the areas of production. In fact, when Christopher Columbus reached the island of Guanaja in 1502, although he had only a limited appreciation of this very bitter sacred drink offered to him by the Aztecs on his arrival, he was quick to exchange other goods for some sacks of cocoa beans.

These three plants were brought back by Western travelers to the courts of Europe by the sixteenth century. They were considered fascinating, exotic products and became luxury beverages, at first prescribed by doctors. Over the course of the centuries they conquered every level of Western society and were by turn demonized and adulated, their consumption alternating between medicinal and pleasurable.

The courts of Europe had divided the world between them and vied with one another to grow these three plants. Plantations were established and moved from one continent to another at the mercy of victories and power struggles between the different European empires – even at this period it is possible to talk about competition. Tea was considered a philosophical drink, coffee more political, and cocoa as divine … and also perhaps the one that appealed most to the senses.

While China preserved its tradition of consuming tea, the tradition of drinking coffee and cocoa was virtually lost in the regions in which the plants originated. Both coffee and cocoa became Western drinks produced in the countries of the south for export, the processing methods becoming industrialized in the consumer countries of the north. The great advantage of tea for producing countries is that it leaves the plantation "finished," and with a certain added value. In the main, coffee and cocoa are still at the raw materials stage when

they leave the producer countries, and are therefore subject to stock-market fluctuations, which is not the case with tea.

Many works have been written about these three plants, the oldest and most famous of which is the *Traités nouveaux et curieux du café, du thé et du chocolate* (*New and Curious Treatises on Coffee, Tea and Chocolate*) written by Philippe Sylvestre Dufour in 1685.

"It is to Arabia that we owe a debt for Coffee and to China that we are indebted for Tea. The taste of both is equally bitter. They became known in Europe at about the same time: both are drunk as hot as can be tolerated, and the experience and the accounts of those who have written of them attribute to them roughly the same effects. There is, however, this notable difference between them, that Coffee is a seed and Tea a leaf … As far as the manner of preparing Tea and consuming it is concerned, there is little difference between it and Coffee, except that Tea being a leaf, and consequently a more open and less solid material than Coffee which is a bean, more easily imparts its color to the water and has less need of being boiled." [1]

	2005 production — millions of tons (FAO data)
Dry tea leaves	3.2
Green coffee	7.7
Cocoa beans	3.9

Bitterness: a taste shared in common

These plants all share a common taste sensation: that of bitterness. To lessen this bitterness, the Arabs and Mayans respectively began roasting coffee beans and cocoa beans, and the Chinese began fixing tea leaves with heat or allowing them to oxidize.

"When Coffee has boiled in milk and has thickened a little … it is similar to the taste of Chocolate, which almost everyone finds good … I have no doubt either that Tea must go very well with milk, as it is bitter like Coffee, and shares many of its qualities."[2]

From spicy soup to a mild and milky drink

In their regions of origin, these bitter drinks were often mixed with spices, salt, and grain flour, turning them into veritable soups. Coffee beans were roasted, ground, then prepared in decoctions, sometimes with the addition of spices such as cloves, cinnamon, and vanilla. Cocoa beans, ground on a stone with a pestle, were then kneaded to form a paste. This paste, diluted in warm water and whisked – known by the Aztecs as *xocoatl* – is what produced chocolate; it would sometimes have vanilla, capsicum, annatto, pepper, cinnamon, or cornmeal added. At the same period, tea was being consumed in the form of a soup, with the addition of spices and other condiments, then whisked. A pinch of salt or pepper could be added to all three drinks, but never sugar. As a result, the bitterness continued to dominate.

As this bitterness did not suit the Western palate, Europeans began to add sugary flavorings (mainly sugar or honey) to these drinks, as well as milk, in order to reduce the bitterness and astringency.

Tonic plants

As soon as they reached Europe, these plants developed a reputation for aiding digestion, making the mind more alert, and purifying the blood. As they belong to the family of plants with tonic properties, they do indeed have energizing qualities due, among other things, to the theine or caffeine contained by all three in variable quantities. A $3^1/_2$-fluid-ounce (100-milliliter) cup of filter coffee may contain between 50 and 175 milligrams; the same quantity of tea between 20 and 70 milligrams; and $3^1/_2$ ounces (100 grams) of dark chocolate between 20 and 200 milligrams. Tea and cocoa have another alkaloid in common, theobromine, which has powerful diuretic properties, cocoa containing far more than tea (0.2 percent in the case of tea leaves, and 2–3 percent in the case of cocoa beans). Both also have powerful antioxidant properties due to their polyphenols, including catechins.

[2] Traités Nouveaux et Curieux du Café, du Thé et du Chocolate: Ouvrage également nécessaire aux médecins et à tous ceux qui aiment leur santé (New and Curious Treatises on Coffee, Tea and Chocolate: A Required Work for both Doctors and Those Who Value Their Health), *op. cit.*

ABOVE :
Roasted coffee beans,
São Tomé.

OPPOSITE :
Wu Yi Da Hong Pao,
Oolong Chinese tea, in a
Chinese teacup with
saucer, La Sensitive, Paris.

to the extent of identifying the estate or garden where the product was harvested. This makes it possible to enjoy specific product types, with their own character, and to offer a far more extensive range of aromas and flavors. At the same time, the blending of *crus* is still important for each of these products. Blending makes it possible to provide a quality product that remains constant throughout the seasons, year upon year, whereas "pure origin" products must be accepted as they are, for their own qualities, whether good or bad.

"Terroir" products

Varieties

The most highly regarded varieties are, in the case of coffee, "arabica"; of cocoa, the modern "criollo"; and of tea, "sinensis." Each plant has a robust variety, which protects against disease, adapts to climatic conditions on lowlands, and has a healthy productivity: "robusta" for coffee (representing 35 percent of production); "forastero" for cocoa (80 percent of production); and "assamica" for tea (40 percent of production).

The concept of "terroir"

These tropical plants thrive in moderate heat – 68 to 77°F (20 to 25°C) – and humidity – rainfall of 60 to 80 inches (1,500 to 2,000 millimeters) per year. Coffee and tea grow better at altitude – up to 6,500 feet (2,000 meters) for coffee; while cocoa is usually happy at altitudes below 2,300 feet (700 meters). However, coffee, like cocoa, grows better in the shade of other plants such as banana trees or erythrinas. All three like deep, well-drained, acid soils.

Pure origins and blends

Since the 1990s, the concept of "purity of origin" – which advocates the notion of "terroir" – has begun to be applied to these three products. Major brands of chocolate, coffee, and tea have begun to highlight origin,

The art of tasting

All three products use the same tasting techniques: visual, olfactory, and gustatory assessment. The terms applied include the following.

☞ For color: cup for coffee; liquor for tea; robe for chocolate.

☞ For aroma: flowery, fruity, burned, spicy, woody aromas.

☞ For taste: balance between acid and bitter for coffee; between bitter and sweet for tea; between acid, bitter, and sweet for chocolate.

☞ For touch: body or full-bodied for coffee or tea; texture for chocolate.

☞ For all three: length in the mouth or aromatic persistence.

SIMILARITIES AND AFFINITIES OF TASTE

Tea, coffee, and cocoa were, to an extent, competitors during the early centuries of their consumption and it is only during recent years, with the effects of globalization and the *world food* trend, that they have started to be combined, either by mixing them together in recipes or by combining them during a meal, one as an ingredient in a dish, the other as a drink to accompany it.

With tea and chocolate there is a true union, the two being combined in the same recipe.

As well as a drink, chocolate is indeed a foodstuff in its own right used as an ingredient in cooking and can therefore become the medium for tea-based recipes. In recent years there has been a fashion for combining origin teas in infusion or powder form with ganaches of white, milk or dark chocolate. A dark chocolate tart flavored with Chinese red Keemun tea is an absolute delight.

In the case of tea and coffee, which have remained in the realm of drinks, it is more a question of complementary qualities and affinities with a particular dish. Foie gras flavored with coffee is exquisite accompanied by a drink of tea.

THE WORLD OF TEA: AN INSPIRATION TO EXPERTS FROM THE WORLD OF CHOCOLATE AND COFFEE

"I love tea in the morning. For me it's a drink that hydrates, that quenches your thirst. I'm very fond of good, strong espresso, but for me coffee is not a hydrating drink. Tea is also far more subtle than coffee. My favorite tea, which I've drunk (very strong) every morning for years, is a red *cru* tea from Yunnan. I find it has aromatic notes suggestive of coffee. Perhaps the reason these two drinks have been at odds is that one of them – tea – is more ritualized in our countries than coffee, so it's not drunk 'on the hoof' in the way coffee is. But they are really complementary during the day, and there's no reason not to be a keen enthusiast of both – there's no contradiction in that." (PIERRE-HENRI MASSIA, *coffeeologist*.)

"I first discovered tea in tea bags. It wasn't until fifteen or so years ago that I discovered whole-leaf teas and the enormous difference between these and tea bags. As with chocolate, I set about discovering tea through methodical tastings, trying to remember and to compare in order to educate my palate. For me, tea as a product is a noble substance not to be consumed in just any old way. One should take one's time preparing it and drinking it. It provides a moment of rest when you want a treat or to gain some quiet relief … Once you've discovered the world of tea, you may well come to associate a certain tea with a certain moment or a certain mood. So there is enormous potential for pleasure! Like chocolate, it's a subtle product that first requires the palate to be educated. Though the potential for enjoying it may be

there, a progression is needed, an apprenticeship to discover its many facets. On the one hand, there is the crescendo of discovery of an entire universe and, at the same time, there is that traumatizing phase when you can no longer step backwards where quality is concerned! In terms of quality, a simple Earl Grey means nothing, just as a 70 percent cocoa solid means nothing." (CHLOË DOUTRE-ROUSSEL, *chocolate buyer*.)

From comparison to combination

TEA-FLAVORED GANACHES

"It must be remembered that for many years chocolate was consumed only in liquid form. It was not until the end of the eighteenth century that the first chocolate in solid form appeared. This was the brainchild of Messieurs Sulpice Debauve and Auguste Gallais who hit on the idea of selling chocolate candies in a medicinal form in Rue des Saints-Pères in Paris. As for ganache – couverture[3] emulsified with liquid cream and possibly butter – it's far more recent, dating back just twenty-five years. Before this, people ate fondant creams, candies made with crystallized orange peel, dried fruit and nuts, pralines, and so on. Candies with a ganache filling are a French creation: it was Maurice Bernachon who, in 1975, produced one filled with a fondant ganache named 'Princesse,' followed by Robert Linxe of La Maison du Chocolat who perfected it. The flavoring of ganaches with plant infusions is very recent indeed. It was Linxe who began it in the 1980s. In the beginning, the only teas used were perfumed teas, such as Earl Grey, jasmine tea,

and Goût Russe, and smoked teas, as there were problems bringing out the flavor of other teas. Nor was there the range of couvertures available today, so the opportunity to create harmonious combinations that were mutually enhancing was more limited. There was also a far more limited knowledge of tea. With the growing fashion for tea that began in France in the 1990s, more combinations were created based on unperfumed teas. It was by learning to understand *grand cru* teas that I discovered that there could be some really interesting combinations between these and *grand cru* chocolate, with each enhancing the flavor of the other." (JACQUES GENIN, *chocolatier*.)

"Tea ganaches are like aromatized teas: in combining these two elements, each is disturbed; the skill is in managing to create a harmony in which each reveals and enhances the other." (CHLOË DOUTRE-ROUSSEL.)

[3] *"Couverture" is the name given to a block of chocolate by those working in the chocolate industry. It is the basic ingredient from which all types of chocolate are made (confectionery, pastries, ganaches, drinking chocolate, and so on).*

FRESH FOIE GRAS POACHED IN A CRUSHED COFFEE BEAN CRUST WITH TRUFFLES AND YUNNAN RED TEA

(Cafés Malongo recipe)

SERVES 8

INGREDIENTS:

☞ lobe fresh foie gras (1lb/500 grams)
☞ 2 ounces/50 grams coffee beans
☞ 1 measure espresso
☞ 2 pints/1 liter red wine
☞ 4 cinnamon sticks
☞ 2 cloves
☞ 1 vanilla bean
☞ Peel of 1 orange
☞ 1 pinch curry powder
☞ 2 star anise
☞ 2 black truffles
☞ peppercorns
☞ coarse Guérande salt

Put the truffles, coffee beans, and espresso in an airtight container. Place in the bottom of the refrigerator for 48 hours: the truffle and coffee aromas will combine.

On the day the dish is to be eaten, prepare a warm wine: pour the red wine into a pan and add the various spices. When the wine comes to a boil, add the extract prepared with the espresso (or make a strong coffee using ground coffee: $3/4$ ounce/20 grams to 2 fluid ounces/7cm^3 of water). Leave on the heat until it returns to boiling point.

Meanwhile, grind the coffee beans and peppercorns separately with a pestle.

Remove the central vein of the foie gras and sprinkle it with the ground coffee and pepper. Roll it up in a cloth to make a sausage shape.

When the wine comes to a boil, remove the pan from the heat and immerse the cloth-wrapped foie gras in it for 15 minutes. If the foie gras is not completely covered by the hot wine, turn it over after 5 minutes.

Take out the foie gras; tighten the cloth and leave it to stand for 1 hour before placing in the bottom of the refrigerator for 2 hours.

To serve, prepare a bed of arugula seasoned with olive oil. Cut the foie gras in to medium slices (about $1/2$ inch/1.5 centimeters), arrange on the arugula, and decorate with slices of truffle and some coarse salt.

To accompany it, choose a powerful, good-quality Yunnan red tea with some astringency and spicy, woody notes, or a smoother Pu-erh black tea with forest and damp moss notes.

DARK CHOCOLATE TART WITH KEEMUN RED TEA

(Recipe by Jacques Génin)

SERVES 8

INGREDIENTS:

For the sugar crust pastry (to be made the day before):
- ☞ 11½ ounces/330 grams flour
- ☞ ½ ounce/15 grams baking powder
- ☞ 12½ ounces/350 grams superfine sugar
- ☞ 1 vanilla bean (deseeded)
- ☞ 1 lb/450 grams softened butter
- ☞ 1 pinch salt
- ☞ 3 eggs

For the ganache:
- ☞ 8 ounces/250 grams + 2 ounces/50 grams good-quality, dark couverture chocolate
- ☞ 8 ounces/250 grams whipping cream plus a little for adding if required
- ☞ 1½ ounces/40 grams superior-quality Keemun red tea

The day before, prepare the tart base. Mix the flour with the baking powder and sugar. Add the vanilla bean, then butter cut into small pieces, and mix. Add the salt, and the eggs whole. Knead the mixture with the palm of the hand. Wrap the pastry dough in plastic wrap and place in the refrigerator overnight.

Roll out the pastry with a little flour but do not overwork it. Blind-bake at 356°F (180°C) in an oven preheated to 410°F (210°C) until golden brown. Melt the couverture chocolate.

When the pastry comes out of the oven, brush it with the melted chocolate and leave to cool. This will prevent the pastry becoming soggy when the ganache filling is poured in.

To make the ganache, bring the cream to a boil. Remove from the heat and infuse the tea in the cream for 3 to 4 minutes.

Strain the infused cream through a sieve, pressing the tea leaves well to extract the maximum liquid. If the volume of the cream has reduced — some may have been absorbed by the tea leaves — adjust the amount to 8 ounces (250 grams) of cream by diluting with milk.

Reheat the cream, but without allowing to boil, and pour it over the couverture chocolate broken into small pieces. Wait for 2 or 3 minutes until the couverture has melted, and blend with a whisk.

Pour the mixture on to the sugar crust pastry base and leave to stand at 54°F (12°C) for a few hours before eating. (Do not place in the refrigerator as this will denature it.)

If any ganache remains, dilute it with milk to make a delicious hot chocolate drink!

Enjoy the tart accompanied by a good-quality Bai Hao Wu Long tea.

TEA AND WINE

Tea and wine are two drinks that have much in common. Competitors in Europe from the seventeenth century, both were initially consumed for their curative powers. The production of both tea and wine is closely associated with the concept of "terroir," their consumption is highly socialized, and the tasting indicators used for both are identical. They can even be drunk together during the course of a meal to bring out their complementary qualities. It is therefore interesting to explore the similarities between them in terms of history, culture, and tasting.

(The quoted text on the following pages is by wine merchant Anne-Marie Rosenberg.)

THE EUROPEAN VINE

Family: Vitaceae or Ampelidaceae
Genus: *Vitis*
Species: *vinifera* (European species originating in Transcaucasia; since the *phylloxera* attack, wine varieties of this species have been grafted on to American rootstock). There are several hundred wine varieties; among the most popular are Chardonnay, Cabernet Sauvignon, Merlot, Sauvignon Blanc, and Pinot Noir.

THE DEVELOPMENT OF RITUALS AND CUSTOMS

From medicine to gastronomy

Like many food products, tea and wine were first associated with medicine before becoming part of the world of gastronomy.

"Hippocrates was the first to recommend wine to treat various illnesses. Later, in the Middle Ages, monasteries continued to prescribe it as a remedy. One amusing example comes from France, where Louis XIV's doctors did battle with him over the advantages of treating him with Burgundy rather than champagne, although the king preferred to drink champagne."

Another anecdote recounts that, having heard that the Chinese and Japanese were great tea drinkers and had no problems with gout or heart disease, Louis XIV began drinking tea regularly. As the king had a very good appetite, his doctor also prescribed tea to aid his digestion.

Social drinking

The drinking of tea and wine is associated with rituals that developed over the course of the centuries; as taste changed, so too did the products that accompanied these drinks – particularly in the case of wine.

"In homage to Dionysus, the Greek god of wine, wine was drunk after the meal in accordance with a highly codified ritual: the hands were washed and made fragrant, and the wine was mixed with water in generous proportions – usually double the quantity of water – and drunk from individual bowls.

"In the Middle Ages, wine was essentially in the hands of the monks and was used as Mass wine but also served to pilgrims who in exchange showed considerable generosity to the monastery. Later, noblemen became more interested in wine as a way of asserting their power. At that time it was not so much a question of wine gastronomy but of a marriage of convenience between the wines and produce of a particular region. People in towns drank wine in taverns; the bourgeoisie drank it at home. The way wine was served had scarcely changed since ancient times: wine was drawn from a cask into pitchers and very often served separately from meals in a shared bowl of

stoneware, pewter, or silver, depending on the wealth of the household. Gradually glass began to be introduced in the form of both bottles and carafes, and Venetian glass replaced the opaque bowls, enhancing the visual qualities of the wine."

The same is true of tea which, from its early beginnings, was consumed in a social manner: on the one hand there was the very strict code followed by members of the emperor's court, which tended toward a refined form of tea drinking, elevating the drink to a gastronomic product; on the other hand there was a more down-to-earth form of tea drinking out in the country, first in the form of soup, with tea being considered a foodstuff, and then as a refreshing drink replacing water that was not suitable for drinking.

From the flavored to the natural

As with tea, other ingredients were also originally added to wine but over the course of history it gradually shed these embellishments and was consumed in its pure form.

"Up to the end of the nineteenth century, water was rarely suitable for drinking, and wine, like vinegar, alcohol, and herbs, was a

ABOVE, FROM LEFT TO RIGHT:
Tea chests, Darjeeling, India; tea is packaged like this for shipping from the tea gardens.

Pinot Noir grapes.

way of purifying it. Wine was rarely consumed neat, and water was never consumed without addition. The unpleasant taste of the wine – which did not store well – was often concealed by the addition of spices.

"Many different combinations were therefore found, including the following.
☞ The Hippocras wine produced in the Middle Ages, which of course originated with Hippocrates; this was a white or red wine combined with honey, cinnamon, ginger, and pepper.
☞ Vermouths, which were a legacy of Greek and Roman flavored wines (usually white wine with sugar or mistelle, alcohol, and aromatic herbs).
☞ The May wine of Germany, a more homely cousin of vermouth: a macerated blend of wine, lemon juice, and woodruff leaves, which contains a lot of coumarin, mint, strawberry, currant, and sparkling water or sparkling wine. Some believe it to be the wine of the druids.
☞ Greek wines salted with seawater.
☞ Smoked wines: wines exposed to heat and, to some extent, to the odor of the smoke itself when placed in smokehouses. This tradition continues with Madeira wines, which are left to age near ovens.

"It was not until the second half of the nineteenth century that wine became considered a foodstuff rather than a medicament. It was then that people began to talk about harmonies between certain dishes and wines. At this period a different wine was drunk with each course. Today we tend to favor a maximum of two wines to accompany an entire meal. Wine gastronomy did not really begin to appear until the 1980s."

TERROR AND COLORS

There are two stages involved in the production of tea and wine:
☞ the work on the land that allows plants to flourish
☞ the "chemical" work of the manufacturing process, or the cave or cellar in which this process occurs.

The concept of terroir

For both tea and wine, the concept of terroir is inextricably bound to the particular character and quality of the finished product. Both are cultivated in accordance with particular climatic conditions. Varieties are chosen to suit a particular terroir and climate. Then comes the work on the vines and in the cellars which, for centuries, was carried out in an empirical manner. The know-how of the wine grower and tea grower is fundamental to their success.

"In the early years of the twelfth century, the monks of Burgundy began to identify areas of vineyard where the soil, situation, and aspect produced wines with particular characteristics. They observed differences in color, body, and aroma. They processed the grapes separately and were able to identify the different 'terres.' By identifying the most characterful wines, they were able to establish the Burgundy 'terroirs.' They then enclosed the best plots with walls, creating the first 'clos.' Thus was born the most famous of all, the twelfth-century Clos Vougeot. A Burgundian legend recounts that the monks even tasted the soil itself to gain a better understanding of it, and chose red or white varieties according to soil characteristics. For example, in the case of Côte de Beaune, planted with a red variety – Pinot Noir – the lower down the hillside, the richer the soil is in iron; the higher, the richer the soil is in clay. This can be seen in the color, with a gray that becomes more intense toward the top of the slopes; the wines grown there are more refined and have a more marked aromatic intensity."

APPETIZER :
SEAFOOD POACHED IN A JAPANESE SENCHA GREEN TEA BROTH

Drink with: Japanese *Sencha* **green tea and** *AOC Pouilly fumé* **wine.**

Why this combination?
Sencha has lively, plant, and marine notes. It is a tea that harmonizes perfectly with any seafood, as it has sufficient aroma and bitterness to balance this type of dish.
Pouilly fumé is a light, but rounded and firm, wine that can be enjoyed young or left to mature.
Variety: made from a single variety, Sauvignon Blanc, also known as "blanc fumé."
Robe: light, pale green.
Nose: bright, floral, musk, spices.
Mouth: very supple, fruity with white fruit flavors (peach, apricot), exotic fruits when older, and a flinty, smoked, gunflint quality. With its length in the mouth, this celebrated wine makes an ideal accompaniment to fish and shellfish.

SERVES 4

PREPARATION TIME : 25 minutes
COOKING TIME : 10 minutes

INGREDIENTS :
- 8 ounces/250 grams shrimps
- 12^1/$_2$ ounces/350 grams scallops
- 1 pint/^{1}/$_2$ liter mussels
- 10^1/$_2$ ounces/300 grams cockles
- 2 ounces/50 grams butter
- 2 sprigs parsley
- 1 shallot
- 4 oysters
- ^{1}/$_2$ teaspoon Japanese *Sencha* green tea
- salt
- pepper
- 3 sprigs fresh cilantro
- 1 teaspoon olive oil

Shell the shrimps, wash the scallops, and dice them. Place the mussels, cockles, butter, whole parsley, and shallot (peeled and chopped) in a large pan. Add a small glass of water and bring to a boil on a low heat, stirring from time to time.

When the shellfish are fully open, drain and shell them. Then strain off the cooking liquid into another pan, leaving the sediment to get rid of any sand.

Steep the tea in the hot liquid. Add the seafood, shellfish and oysters with their juices. Season with salt and pepper, cover and leave to "cook" for 5 minutes in the warm liquid.

Arrange the seafood in individual bowls, pour the liquid over, add a few cilantro leaves and a drizzle of olive oil. Eat while warm, but not too hot, accompanied by iced *Sencha* tea and/or *Pouilly fumé*.

In China, the siting of tea plantations is decided according to *feng shui* principles, which take ambient energy flows into account. The aim is to find the best aspect and the best-drained soil to ensure the tea plants flourish. Different varieties of tea bush are planted depending on the soil and climate. Also, as time goes by, tea plants adapt to the different ecosystems, producing what are called ecotypes, that is to say, varieties very close to the original variety but with certain slightly different gustatory characteristics. Vines prefer chalky or clay-and-chalk soils, whereas tea bushes grow best on acid soils. However, both plants thrive best on hillsides or mountainsides. As they grow older, both tea plants and vines develop deeper and deeper roots that allow them to draw from the depths of the soil the mineral elements typical of each terroir – the "very substance of each 'terre.'" It is this gradual symbiosis with the terroir that makes tea plants and vines improve with age: old vines, like old tea plants, are sought after for their aromatic potential, and are processed separately. For example, in Yunnan, one of the regions of the world where tea originated, some wild tea plants many centuries old are still harvested, and the resulting tea fetches very high prices. Vines and tea plants thrive in different climates – vines like temperate climates, whereas tea plants grow best in humid, tropical conditions – although both are perennials and relatively hardy, tolerating a wide range of temperatures.

The terroir gives expression to the variety

"In the United States, too, the characteristics of different terroirs have been exploited, producing excellent Pinot Noir wines in the cold areas of California, such as the Carneros region famous for its cold mists, and Oregon, which receives a lot of rain. In Oregon there are also some Burgundy varieties that produce great red wines for the American market."

The concept of "varieties" also applies to tea cultivation. Different varieties are chosen depending on the region, the terroir, and the desired tea color. In Japan, in particular, the jade-green color of the leaves is a very important quality criterion, and the varieties used are very rich in chlorophyll. In China, the well-known Keemun estates produce a red tea from the Mao Feng variety normally used to produce green tea. This gives more fruity and flowery notes in the cup and a reduction in the leather and woody notes.

Wine colors, tea colors

Tea leaves, like grapes, must be speedily transported to the processing site or they will spoil. Just as white, rosé, or red wine can be produced from black grapes depending on the production process used, so green tea leaves can produce the six tea colors already mentioned. As with wine, particular regions specialize in the production of particular colors of tea. However, no system as codified or strict as the AOC (Appellation d'Origine Contrôlée) exists to restrict the varieties or processing methods used. This allows greater freedom to experiment and explore in order to meet demand, and permits a certain flexibility to adapt to the market. But the finest and most highly regarded cru teas are the result of processes that are sometimes centuries old. Although still very much in its early stages – except in China – the development of an AOC system has begun, so that tea-growing areas can protect and preserve their quality image. In India, notably, there are three AOC

types – Darjeeling, Assam, and Nilgiri – each of which has its own logo certifying the origin of the tea. This system was set up by the Tea Board of India to guard against imitations. For example, ten times more Darjeeling tea is drunk worldwide than is produced in Darjeeling! It is through specializing, respecting the symbioses between terroir and tea variety, and learning to master the different stages of processing that the very finest cru teas are produced. If one were to compare the colors of tea and wine, one would liken oxidized tea – the more oxidized the tea is, the more full-bodied it becomes, because of the polymerization of the tannins – to red wines, which capture the tannins in the grape skin. White wine is closer to green tea, although green tea does contain tannins, unlike white wine, except when it has been stored in casks.

(Recipe by Jean-François Mallet)

MAIN COURSE:
GLAZED FILLET OF DUCK BREAST WITH INDIAN ASSAM SPRING RED TEA, CELERIAC, AND APPLE PURÉE

Drink with: Indian *Assam Spring* red tea and *AOC Cornas, Cave de Tain L'Hermitage* wine.

Why this combination?
Assam Spring is a powerful tea with astringency and a fine full body. Spring gives it flowery, tobacco, and woody aromatic notes that harmonize wonderfully well with a seasoned red meat such as fillet of duck breast.
The young *Cornas* wine is slightly bitter, but as it ages it gains in power, roundness, and suppleness.
Variety: Syrah.
Robe: dark, almost black.
Nose: pepper, spices, leather, game, cocoa, blackcurrant, toast.
Mouth: Full-flavored with powerful tannins; the same notes as found in the nose with some noticeable earthy and forest notes. The Syrah variety becomes wild and peppery with hints of candied fruit.

SERVES 4

PREPARATION TIME: 40 minutes
COOKING TIME: 30 minutes

INGREDIENTS:
- 10^1/$_2$ ounces/300 grams celeriac
- 3 Golden Delicious apples
- 2 ounces/50 grams butter
- 2 duck breast fillets
- 2 teaspoons honey
- 4 teaspoons soy sauce
- 2 teaspoons Indian *Assam Spring* red tea
- 1 cup liquor from the same tea
- salt
- pepper

Peel the celeriac, cut into pieces, and cook in a pan of salted boiling water. Drain and rinse under running cold water and dry with a cloth.

Peel and cut the apples into quarters. Melt the butter in a frying pan, seal the apple quarters in the hot butter, and leave on a low heat to take color. Add the pieces of celeriac and leave to soften together for 3 minutes. Season with salt and pepper, and mash the apples and celeriac roughly with a fork; set aside.

Remove the fat from the duck fillets and begin cooking them on a low heat, skin side down, in a non stick frying pan. When they are golden brown, turn them over and cook them on the other side for 3 minutes, then turn them out to drain on a plate and leave to rest.

Degrease the pan, add the honey, and allow it to caramelize. Add the soy sauce and leave to reduce for 1 minute before adding the tea liquor.

When the reduction has thickened, turn off the heat and add the tea leaves. Allow the tea to steep for a few minutes in the sauce, then adjust the seasoning with salt and pepper.

Cut the breasts into thick slices; add any juices to the sauce.

Arrange the duck slices and the celeriac-and-apple mixture on a large dish or on individual plates. Pour over the tea sauce, and enjoy with a hot *Assam Spring* tea and/or a *Cornas, Cave de Tain L'Hermitage* wine.

SIMILARITIES AND AFFINITIES OF TASTE

Tea and wine: two worlds of taste – one based on water, the other on alcohol – that require a similar approach. The theine (caffeine) or alcohol they contain means that both are masticated and then expelled during tasting sessions.

"There is a genuine parallel between each of these two products in the mouth: the same reaction to bitter, sweet, salty, and sour and in retro-olfaction."

The vocabulary is the same, with certain flavors or aromatic families being evident in both to a greater or lesser extent, depending on the tea or wine.

"The only taste sensation I found to be more marked in certain teas is salt. Where aromas are concerned, I found that teas contain families of aromas often present in wine, such as red fruits and wood, particularly pronounced in certain Parkerized Bordeaux-type wines."

On the other hand, certain aromatic families that are common and frequent in tea are far less so in wine, for example the family of marine notes (oyster, seaweed, fish).

Exploring tea and wine affinities around a menu

"Today, when people have health problems and can no longer drink wine (or at least must reduce their consumption), yet still wish to explore interesting harmonies as part of a refined cuisine, I believe that tea can be a genuine substitute if the pursuit of harmony is conducted with the same sensitivity as it is with wine."

Tea is traditionally drunk outside mealtimes, but the similarities it offers with wine means that it can also be consumed with meals.

BELOW:
Exploring the affinity
between Bai Hao Wu
Long *"Oriental Beauty"*
and AOC Marsannay 2002
(Pinot Noir vine, Domaine
Dominique Laurent) Chai
33, Paris.

DESSERT:
FRUIT POACHED IN AN INFUSION OF INDIAN DARJEELING SUMMER RED TEA

Drink with: Indian *Darjeeling Summer* red tea and *Jurançon Wine*.

Why this combination?
Darjeeling Summer has woody, flowery notes and is generally a tea that is bright in the mouth with a certain astringency and bitterness that accords perfectly with sweet dishes, particularly fruits.
Jurançon is a mellow wine.
Principal varieties: Petit Manseng and Gros Manseng.
Robe: bright and golden.
Nose: vanilla, mild spices, honey, candied fruits, cream.
Mouth: fleshy, highly perfumed, sometimes slightly spicy with cinnamon, clove, honey, beeswax, candied fruits, brown sugar, mild spices, vanilla, cream, candied pineapple; below its apparent sweetness lies a vivacity that gives it freshness and balance. There are also exotic fruit notes, depending on the ripeness of the grapes.

SERVES 4

PREPARATION TIME: 25 minutes
COOKING TIME: 20 minutes

INGREDIENTS:
- 1 lb/500 grams superfine sugar
- 2 peaches
- 4 apricots
- 4 teaspoons of *Darjeeling Summer* red tea
- juice of ¹/₂ a lemon
- ¹/₂ a vanilla bean

Make a syrup by boiling the sugar in 1 pint (¹/₂ liter) of water for 20 minutes on a low heat. Wash the fruit and poach it in the syrup separately: 10 minutes for the peaches, 5 minutes for the apricots. Drain carefully and peel them with the point of a knife. Split them in half and arrange with care in a salad bowl. Pour over the warm syrup to cover the fruit, then add the tea, the lemon juice, and the lightly grated vanilla bean.

Leave to cool, then place in the refrigerator. Serve very cold with a hot Indian *Darjeeling Summer* red tea and/or *Jurançon* wine.

TEA AND PERFUME

FRAGRANT TEA

The fragrant quality of tea has always taken precedence over its aroma and taste. Ten years ago, tea made its entry into the world of perfumery where it is increasingly making its mark as an element of evocation in some of the great perfumes.

"Japanese tea, invariably served without milk or sugar, which would be harmful to its aroma, is the most mellow, most agreeable drink that one could be given to taste … Gyokuro, for example, which is the most highly regarded tea in Uji and throughout Japan, instills into its flavor such balsamic subtleties that it more resembles a perfume; it is as if some marvelous alchemy has succeeded in liquefying the aromas of flowers – garden flowers, wild flowers – transferring the pleasure of smell to that of taste. Such is gyokuro."

LE CULTE DU THÉ (THE CULT OF TEA), WENCESLAU DE MORALES, 1905, PUBLISHED BY LA DIFFÉRENCE, 1998

Tea is one of those rare products of taste that man has thought to associate with the evocative flower world of perfume. The Chinese began perfuming tea leaves with flower petals long ago to enhance their aromatic bouquet. Then, in the 1970s, the fashion for aromatized teas only served to highlight the entry of perfume into the world of tea.

TEA PERFUMES

The entry of tea into the world of perfume is recent – dating only from the 1990s. At first it was green tea, synonymous with purity and with its fresh, herbaceous, plant notes, that enjoyed immediate success during these early years. Then it was perfumed teas such as Earl Grey, Goût Russe, and jasmine tea that inspired great new creations, along with smoked tea. An increasingly refined understanding of the olfactory world of tea has led perfumers on a quest for new inspiration, enriched of course by the extensive palette of fragrances available in nonaromatized "origin" teas.

"Tea allows me to drink the fragrances that fascinate me and with which I create perfumes. Tea is in fact a perfume that we drink; so I've been able to experience what it is to drink flowers! And the most sublime flowers, fresher than in nature, such as peony, lily of the valley, lilac, but I have also been able to drink wood, leather, earth. There is no difference between a tea and a perfume. Both are fragrant liquids. One is a perfect harmony constructed by nature; the other a quest for perfect harmony pursued by humankind. But both contain the same diversity, a very extensive olfactory range. Tea and perfume are fragrant liquids. One is drunk; the other scents. But, after all, if tea is a perfume that is drunk, why should we not scent ourselves with a drop of infused tea? Why not wear the woody notes of a Keemun tea, the leathery, smoky notes of a Lapsang Souchong, or the beautiful lilac and peony notes of a Bao Zhong tea? Tea is a constant source of inspiration, but also of emulation. I endeavor to equal the fineness of these aromatic notes. I have worked with tea a great deal as a leading element in my creations, but not as an ingredient because the essence or 'absolute' of tea leaves, when one finds it, in no sense reproduces the true note of infused tea leaves.[4] It is more a source of inspiration when seeking to recreate these magnificent notes and to give the impression of smelling a cup of tea in the final fragrance. There is no difference between tea and perfume, and indeed certain perfumed teas are named after perfumes and could lead you to believe that they had been blended with perfume. What is a tea perfumed with citrus? An eau-de-cologne tea! One can truthfully say that tea is in fact perfume."

(MATHILDE LAURENT, *perfumer.*)

ABOVE, FROM LEFT TO RIGHT:
Phial of perfume or essential oils for aromatized tea?

Rosebuds, often combined with red tea in perfumed teas in China.

The fragrance of Goût Russe tea or Eau de Cologne?

[4] *In perfumery, what is referred to as the "tea" note is in fact the maté absolute, which has tobacco, herbaceous, and hay notes (see page 58, chapter I, "A History of Tea").*

A TIMELINE OF TEA IN PERFUMERY

A short list	Year	Evocation	
Eau parfumée, Bulgari	1992	green tea	
Thé pour un été, L'Artisan parfumeur	1996	green tea	
Eau de Camellia chinois, Maître parfumeur et Gantier	1997	green tea	
Black, Bulgari	1998	red tea	
Eau de thé vert, Roger et Gallet	2000	green tea	
Green Tea, Elizabeth Arden	2000	green tea	
Series 1, Leaves: TEA, Comme des garçons	2000	smoked tea	
Tea for Two, L'Artisan parfumeur	2000	smoked tea	
Spiced Green Tea, Elizabeth Arden	2001	chai tea	
Eau parfumée au thé blanc, Bulgari	2003	white tea	
Thé vert, L'Occitane	2005	green tea	

OPPOSITE:
*Jasmine flowers, the first
combination shared by tea
and perfume, dating from
the Chinese Tang dynasty.*

V ADDRESS BOOK

A short world tour of enchanting tea rooms and tea merchants to visit on every continent ... and just around the corner.

For example, immediately on the right is the entrance to the Kusmi Russian tea house in Avenue Niel, Paris. Opposite is Mademoiselle Li's Chinese tea salon, also in Paris.

SPECIALIST TEA ROOMS AND TEA MERCHANTS IN THE GREAT CAPITAL CITIES OF THE WORLD

TR stands for Tea Room (where you can enjoy drinking tea)
TM stands for Tea Merchant (where you can buy tea to brew at home)

EUROPE

BELGIUM

Brussels

☞ COMPTOIR FLORIAN
TM and TR
17 Rue Saint-Boniface 1050
Tel: +32 2 513 91 03

☞ LA MAISON DU THÉ
TM
11 Rue Plattesteen 1000
Tel: +32 2 512 32 26

☞ LA SEPTIÈME TASSE
TM and TR
www.7etasse.com
37 Rue du Bailli 1050
Tel: +32 2 647 19 71

☞ LE PALAIS DES THÉS
TM
45 Place de la Vieille-Halle-aux-Blés 1000
Tel: +32 2 502 45 59

☞ UNIVERS DU THÉ
TM
14 Rue Podenbrock (Grand Sablon) 1000
Tel: +32 2 513 20 67

FRANCE

Paris

1ST ARRONDISSEMENT

☞ L'UNIVERSITÉ DU THÉ
ET LE CLUB DES BUVEURS DU THÉ
Tea tastings and talks
www.clubdesbuveursdethe.org
IESA, 5 Avenue de l'Opéra 75001
Tel: +331 49 11 47 70
Metro station: Pyramides or Palais-Royal-Musée du Louvre

☞ TORAYA
Japanese TR
10 Rue Saint-Florentin 75001
Tel: +331 42 60 13 00
Metro station: Concorde

4TH ARRONDISSEMENT

☞ MARIAGE FRÈRES – MARAIS
TM and TR
www.mariagefreres.com
30 Rue du Bourg-Tibourg 75004
Tel: +331 42 72 28 11
Metro station: Hôtel-de-Ville or Saint-Paul

5TH ARRONDISSEMENT

☞ LA MAISON DES TROIS THÉS
Chinese TM and TR
33 Rue Gracieuse 75005
Tel: +331 43 36 93 84
Metro station: Monge

☞ LA MOSQUÉE DE PARIS
TR serving mint tea
2 Place du Puits-de-l'Ermite 75005
Tel: +331 45 35 97 33
Metro station: Censier-Daubenton

☞ PÂTISSERIE SADAHARU AOKI
Specialists in maccha confectionery
www.sadaharuaoki.com
56 Boulevard Port Royal 75005
Tel: +331 45 35 36 80 / Fax: 01 45 35 34 13
RER station: Port-Royal

☞ TASHI DELEK
Tibetan restaurant serving salted milk tea
4 Rue des Fossés-Saint-Jacques 75005
Tel: +331 43 26 55 55
RER station: Luxembourg

☞ TEA CADDY
British TR
14 Rue Saint-Julien-le-Pauvre 75005
Tel: +331 43 54 15 56
Metro station: Saint-Michel

☞ THÉS DE CHINE
Chinese TM and TR
Information center on the art of Chinese tea (tea tastings and talks)<P>
20 Boulevard Saint-Germain 75005
Tel: +331 40 46 98 89
Metro station: Maubert-Mutualité

6TH ARRONDISSEMENT

☞ L'ARTISAN DE SAVEURS
TR
www.lartisandesaveurs.com
72 Rue du Cherche-Midi 75006
Tel: +331 42 22 46 64
Metro station: Sèvres-Babylone or Saint-Placide

☞ LA MAISON DE LA CHINE
Chinese TM and TR
76 Rue Bonaparte 75006
Tel: +331 40 51 95 16
Metro station: Saint-Sulpice

☞ L'HEURE GOURMANDE
Cozy TR
22 Passage Dauphine 75006
Tel: +331 46 34 00 40
Metro station: Odéon

☞ MALONGO CAFÉ
TM, TR, and café
www.malongo.com
50 Rue Saint-André-des-Arts 75006
Tel: +331 43 26 47 10 / Fax: 01 53 10 87 88
Metro station: Odéon or Saint-Michel

☞ MARIAGE FRÈRES – RIVE GAUCHE
TM and TR
13 Rue des Grands-Augustins 75006
Tel: +331 40 51 82 50
Metro station: Odéon

☞ PÂTISSERIE SADAHARU AOKI
Specialists in maccha *confectionery*
www.sadaharuaoki.com
35 Rue de Vaugirard 75006
Tel: +331 45 44 48 90 / Fax: 01 45 44 48 29
Metro station: Rennes or Saint-Placide

7TH ARRONDISSEMENT

☞ PEGOTY'S
TR
79 Avenue Bosquet 75007
Tel: +331 45 55 84 50
Metro station: École Militaire

8TH ARRONDISSEMENT

☞ BERNARDAUD
TR
9 Rue Royale 75008
Tel: +331 42 66 22 55
Metro station: Concorde

☞ FAUCHON
TM and TR (tea tastings and talks)
26–30 Place de la Madeleine 75008
Tel: +331 47 42 90 10
Metro station: Madeleine

☞ HÉDIARD
TM and TR
21 Place de la Madeleine 75008
Tel: +331 43 12 88 88
Metro station: Madeleine

☞ HÔTEL LE BRISTOL
TR
11 Rue du Faubourg-Saint-Honoré 75008
Tel: +331 53 43 43 42
Metro station: Champs-Élysées-Clemenceau

☞ MARIAGE FRÈRES – ÉTOILE
TM and TR
260 Faubourg Saint-Honoré 75008
Tel: +331 46 22 18 54
Metro station: Ternes or Charles-de-Gaulle-Étoile

☞ MINAMOTO KITCHOAN
Japanese TR
www.kitchoan.com
17 Place de la Madeleine 75008
Tel: +331 40 06 91 28
Metro station: Madeleine

11TH ARRONDISSEMENT

☞ PÂTISSERIE TESNIME
Algerian TR
207 Rue du Faubourg-Saint-Antoine
Tel: +331 43 48 60 97
Metro station: Faidherbe-Chaligny

13TH ARRONDISSEMENT

☞ L'EMPIRE DES THÉS
Chinese TM and TR
101 Avenue d'Ivry 75013
Tel: +331 45 85 66 33
Metro station: Tolbiac

☞ L'OISIVETHÉ
TM and TR
1 Rue Jean-Marie-Jégo 75013
Tel: +331 53 80 31 33
Metro station: Corvisart

15TH ARRONDISSEMENT

☞ JACQUES GENIN, FONDEUR EN CHOCOLAT
Laboratory (no store: call before coming)
Villa Paolini, 18 Rue Saint-Charles 75015
Tel/Fax: +331 45 77 29 01
Metro station: La Motte-Picquet-Grenelle

16TH ARRONDISSEMEN

☞ MADEMOISELLE LI
Chinese TR
Jardin d'Acclimatation
Bois de Boulogne 75016
Tel: +331 40 67 91 55
Metro station: Les Sablons

Bordeaux

☞ CHRIS'TEAS L'INSTANT THÉ
TM and TR
16 Passage Sarget 33000
Tel: +335 56 81 29 86

☞ L'HEURE DU THÉ
TM and TR
20 Rue des Piliers-de-Tutelle 33000
Tel: +335 56 52 49 79

☞ SALON DE THÉ DES REMPARTS
TM and TR
19 Rue des Remparts 33000
Tel: +335 56 90 03 03

Lille

☞ CHA YUAN
TM and TR
8 Rue Saint-Jacques 59000
Tel: +333 28 52 43 70

Lyons

2ND ARRONDISSEMENT

☞ CHA YUAN
TM and TR
www.cha-yuan.com
Also shops in other French towns
7–9 Rue des Remparts-d'Ainay 69002
Tel: +334 72 41 04 60
Metro station: Bellecour

☞ SIMPLE SIMON
British TR
13 Rue Thomassin 69002
Tel: +334 72 41 04 98
Metro station: Cordeliers

Marseilles

1ST ARRONDISSEMENT

☞ LES ARCENAULX
TR and TM
25 Cours Honoré-d'Estienne-d'Orves 13001
Tel: +334 91 54 89 08

6TH ARRONDISSEMENT

☞ SHAMBHALA
TR
40 Rue des Trois-Frères-Barthélemy 13006
Tel: +334 91 47 68 03

Nantes

☞ AU BONHEUR DES THÉS
TM and TR
1 Rue de Verdun 44000
Place de la Cathédrale-Saint-Pierre-et-Saint-
Paul
Tel: +332 40 12 03 32

Strasbourg

☞ AU FOND DU JARDIN
TM and TR
6 Rue de la Rape 67000
Tel: +333 88 24 50 06

Toulouse

☞ ARRÊT FACULTATIF
TM and TR
29 Avenue Étienne-Billières 31300
Tel: +335 61 59 30 58
Metro station: Saint-Cyprien-République

☞ L'AUTRE SALON DE THÉ
TR
45 Rue des Tourneurs 31000
Tel: +335 61 22 11 63
16 Place Saint-Georges 31000
Tel: +335 61 23 46 67
Metro station: Esquirol

☞ LE SHERPA
TR and crêperie
46 Rue du Taur 31000
Tel: +335 61 23 89 29
Metro station: Capitole

GERMANY
Hamburg

Hamburg is one of the largest ports for
Western tea imports. Major tea importers who
set up business in the city after the opening of
the Suez Canal in 1869 still have premises
there. It is tea merchants rather than tea rooms
that are found in the city as tea is mainly
drunk in the big hotels.

☞ CLAUS KRÖGER
TM
Große Bergstr. 241, 22767
Tel: +49 3 80 60 60 / Fax: +40 3 80 60 60

☞ COMPAGNIE COLONIAL
TM
Große Bleichen 12–14, 20354
Tel: +49 35 71 95 62 / Fax: +40 35 71 01 87

☞ DER TEELADEN
TM
Gerhofstr. 27, 20354
Tel: +49 3 48 06 20 / Fax: +40 35 71 82 30

☞ TEE-MAASS
TM
Börsenbrücke 2a, 20457
Tel: +49 3 74 24 74 / Fax: +40 3 89 51 12

IRELAND
Dublin

☞ THE SHELBOURNE HOTEL
TR serving traditional afternoon tea
www.shelbourne.ie
27 St Stephen's Green, Dublin 2
Tel: +353 (0)1 663 4500
Fax: +353 (0)1 661 6006

ITALY
Florence

☞ HEMINGWAY
TR
Piazza Piattelina 9/R 50124
Tel: +39 05 52 84 781

Milan

☞ ARTE DEL RICEVERE
TM
www.artedelricevere.com
Via Macedonio Melloni, 35 – 20219 Milan
Tel: +39 02 28 26 293

SPAIN
Madrid

☞ BOMEC EL PALADAR DEL TÉ
TM and TR
www.bomec-elpaladardelte.com
c/ San Joaquín, 8 – 28004 Madrid
Tel: +34 91 531 16 15

SWITZERLAND
Geneva

☞ L'AMI THÉ
TM
3 Rue de la Terrassière 1207
Tel: +41 (22) 786 05 21

☞ LA SIXIÈME HEURE
TR
Place des Philosophes 1205
Tel: +41 (22) 320 73 69

☞ TSCHIN-TA-NI
TM
5 Rue Verdaine 1211, Geneva 3
Tel: +41 (22) 732 93 72

TURKEY
Istanbul

☞ PIYERLOTI KAHVESI
(PIERRE LOTI CAFÉ)
TR
One of Istanbul's best-known *çay bahcesi*
(tea rooms). It was from here that Pierre
Loti looked out on the Golden Horn.

UNITED KINGDOM
Dumfries

☞ ABBEY COTTAGE TEA ROOMS
TR for traditional afternoon tea
www.abbeycottagetearoom.com
26 Main Street, New Abbey, Dumfries DG2 8BY
Tel: +44 (0)1387 850377

Ely

☞ PEACOCKS
TR for traditional afternoon tea
Email: tea@thepeacocks.co.uk
65 Waterside, Ely, Cambs. CB7 4AU
Tel: +44 (0)1353 661100

Glasgow

☞ THE WILLOW TEAROOMS
TR for traditional afternoon tea
www.willowtearooms.co.uk
217 Sauchiehall Street, Glasgow G2 3EX
Tel: +44 (0)141 3320521

Harlech

☞ CEMLYN RESTAURANT AND TEA SHOP
TR
www.cemlynrestaurant.co.uk
High Street, Harlech, Gwynedd LL46 2YA
Tel: +44 (0)1766 780425

Harrogate

BETTYS CAFÉ TEA ROOMS
TR and TM
www.bettysandtaylors.co.uk
1 Parliament Square, Harrogate,
North Yorkshire HG1 2QU
Tel: +44 (0)1423 877300

Ledbury

☞ **MRS MUFFINS TEASHOP**
TR
1 Church Lane, Ledbury,
Herefordshire HR8 1DL
Tel: +44 (0)1531 633579

London

☞ **BRAMAH MUSEUM OF TEA AND COFFEE**
Museum
www.bramahmuseum.co.uk
40 Southwark Street, London SE1 1UN
Tel / Fax: +44 (0)20 7403 5650
Underground station: London Bridge

☞ **FORTNUM & MASON**
TM and TR
www.fortnumandmason.com
181 Piccadilly, London W1A 1ER
Tel: +44 (0)20 7734 8040
Fax: +44 (0)20 7437 3278
Underground station: Piccadilly Circus or
Green Park

☞ **FOUR SEASONS HOTEL**
TR serving traditional afternoon tea
Named "London's 2003 Top Tea Place of the
Year" by the Tea Council
www.fourseasons.com
Hamilton Place, Park Lane, London W1A 1AZ
Tel: +44 (0)20 7499 0888
Fax: +44 (0) 7493 1895
Underground station: Hyde Park Corner

☞ **LANESBOROUGH HOTEL**
TR serving traditional high tea in the afternoon
www.lanesborough.com
Hyde Park Corner, London SW1X 7TA
Tel: +44 (0)20 7259 5599
Fax: +44 (0)20 7259 5606
Underground station: Hyde Park Corner

☞ **RITZ HOTEL**
Palm Court Tea Room TR
www.theritzlondon.com
150 Piccadilly, London W1J 9BR
Tel: +44 (0)20 7493 8181
Fax: +44 (0)20 7493 2687
Underground station: Green Park

☞ **TWININGS STRAND SHOP**
TM Original Twinings shop since 1717
216 The Strand, London WC2R 1AP
Tel: +44 (0)20 7353 3511
Underground station: Temple

☞ **YAUATCHA**
Restaurant
15–17 Broadwick Street, Soho, London
W1F 0DL
Tel: +44 (0)20 7494 8888
Underground station: Oxford Circus

Ollerton

☞ **OLLERTON WATERMILL TEA**
TR for traditional afternoon tea
Market Place, Ollerton,
Newark NG22 9AA
Tel: +44 (0)1623 822469

Penrith

☞ **NEW VILLAGE TEA ROOMS**
TR for traditional afternoon tea
Orton, Penrith, Cumbria CA10 3RH
Tel: +44 (0)1539 624886

Truro

☞ **CHARLOTTE'S TEA HOUSE**
TR for traditional afternoon tea
Email: teahouse@btconnect.com
Coinage Hall, 1 Boscawen Street, Truro,
Cornwall TR1 2QU
Tel: +44 (0)1872 263706

AFRICA

In Africa, particularly in north and west
Africa, you are likely to be offered tea to drink
when you enter a store as well as on the street.
Tea is the drink enjoyed by everyone at any
time of day, and this is why – with the
exception of Morocco, where the tradition of
mint tea originated – no other country is listed.
However, as in Asia, people living in the tea-
producing countries – mainly in central and
east Africa – only drink tea occasionally; in fact
it is often difficult to find good-quality tea to
drink in these countries as the crop is destined
for export.

MOROCCO

Marrakesh

☞ **HÔTEL LA MAMOUNIA**
TR / restaurant
www.mamounia.com
Avenue Bab Jdid
Tel: +212 (0)44 38 86 00
Fax: +212 (0)44 44 49 / +212 (0)44 44 46 60

☞ **RIAD DAR MOHA**
TR / restaurant
81 Rue Dar El Bacha, Medina
Tel: +212 (0)44 38 64 00
Fax: +212 (0)44 38 69 98
darmoha@iam.net.ma

☞ **RIAD TAMSNA**
TR / restaurant
23 Riad Zitoun Jdid, Derb Zanka Daika
Tel: +212 (0)44 38 52 72
(book in advance for tea)
Fax: +212 (0)44 38 52 71

SOUTH AMERICA

BRAZIL

Rio de Janeiro

☞ **CONFEITARIA COLOMBO**
TR
www.confeitariacolombo.com.br
Praça Coronel Eugênio Franco, 1
– Copacabana Rio de Janeiro
Tel: +55 21 2521 1032

☞ **LIVRARIA DA TRAVESSA**
TR / bookstore
www.travessa.com.br
Rua Visconde de Pirajá, 572
– Ipanema Rio de Janeiro
Tel: +55 21 3205 9002

NORTH AMERICA

CANADA

Montreal

☞ **BETJEMAN & BARTON**
TM
5131 Sherbrooke Ouest (corner of Vendôme)
Tel: +1 514 369 9011

☞ **CAMELLIA SINENSIS**
TM and TR
www.camellia-sinensis.com
347–351 Rue Emery
Tel: +1 514 286 4002

UNITED STATES

EAST COAST

New York

☞ ALICE'S TEA CUP
TR and TM
102 West 73rd Street, New York
Tel: +1 212 799 3006

☞ HEARTBEAT
Restaurant
W Hotel
149 East 49th Street, NY 10017-1202
Tel: +1 212 407 2900

☞ TEANY
Vegetarian restaurant owned by Moby
www.teany.com
90 Rivington Street, NY 1002
Tel: +1 212 475 9190

☞ FOUR SEASONS HOTEL
TR
57 East 57th Street, NY 10021
Tel: +1 212 758 5700

☞ T SALON & T EMPORIUM
TR
11 East 20th Street, NY 10012
Tel: +1 212 358 05 06

☞ WILD LILY TEA ROOM
TR
www.wildlilytearoom.com
511 West 22nd Street, NY 10011-1109
Tel: +1 212 691 2258

Pennsylvania

☞ THE GILBERTSVILLE TEA ROOM
TR
www.thegilbertsvilletearoom.com/
1259 East Philadelphia Avenue, Gilbertsville
Pennsylvania
Tel: +1 610 369 0678

Washington

☞ CHING CHING CHA
TR
1063 Wisconsin Avenue NW, DC 20007
Tel: +1 202 333 8288

☞ TEAISM
TR and TM
www.teaism.com
400 8th Street DC 20004
Tel: +1 202 638 6010

MIDWEST

Chicago

☞ THE RITZ-CARLTON CHICAGO
(A FOUR SEASONS HOTEL)
Hotel
160 E. Pearson Street, Chicago
Tel.: +1 312 266 1000

Illinois

☞ INFINI-TEA
TR
902 Main Street, Antioch, Illinois
Tel: +1 847 395 3520

Minnesota

☞ LADY ELEGANT'S TEA ROOM AND GIFT
SHOP
TR
www.ladyelegantstea.com/
Historic Milton Square, 2230 Carter Avenue,
St. Paul, Minnesota
Tel: +1 651 645 6676

Oklahoma

☞ TEA AT TIVOL INN
TR
1403 W. Washington Place (91st Street),
Oklahoma
Tel: +1 918 449 8648

SOUTH

Florida

☞ LEA'S TEA ROOM & CAFÉ
TR
Bal Harbour Shops, 9700 Collins Avenue,
Bal Harbour, Florida
Tel.: +1 305 868 0901

Texas

☞ TEA EMBASSY
TR and TM
900 Rio Grande Street, Austin, Texas
Tel: +1 512 330 9991

WEST COAST

Los Angeles

☞ CHADO TEA HOUSE
TR
8422-1/2 West Third Street, CA 90048-4112
Tel: +1 323 655 2056

☞ LE PALAIS DES THÉS
TM
401 North Canyon Drive, Beverly Hills,
CA 90210
Tel: +1 310 271 7922

San Francisco

☞ CELADON
Tea bar
www.celadontea.com
1111 Solano Avenue, Albany, CA 94706
Tel: +1 510 524 1696

☞ IMPERIAL TEA COURT
Tea house
www.imperialtea.com
1411 Powell Street, CA, 94133
Tel: +1 415 788 6080 or +1 800 567 5898

☞ LOVEJOY'S ENGLISH TEA ROOM
TR
1351 Church Street, CA 94114
Tel: +1 415 648 5895

☞ SAMOVAR TEA LOUNGE
TR
www.samovartea.com
498 Sanchez Street, CA 94114
Tel: +1 415 626 4700

ASIA

In the countries of the Near and Middle East,
as in Africa, the best way to drink tea is on the
street from small booths. The same is true of
India: on the street, samovars are filled with
tea and you can buy *chai* to drink in glasses or
terracotta bowls.

MAINLAND CHINA

Beijing (Peking)

☞ LAO SHE CHA GUAN
(LAO SHE TEA HOUSE)
Traditional tea house with Peking opera
www.laosheteahouse.com/en/1.htm
Qianmen Xi Dajie, Bldg 3, 3rd floor,
(near the south exit of Tiananmen Square)
Tel: +86 (0)10 6304 6334;
+86 (0)10 6303 6830

Chengdu

Chengdu is China's most prolific city of tea
houses – there are probably more than 1,000!
According to a popular saying, "China has the
best tea houses in the world and Chengdu has
the best tea houses in China." One of the oldest,
dating from the twentieth century, is the YUELAI
tea house, Huaxing Street, in the city center.

Hong Kong

☞ FLAGSTAFF HOUSE MUSEUM OF TEA WARE
Museum
10 Cotton Tree Drive, Hong Kong Park
Tel: +852 2869 0690

☞ LOCK CHA TEA SHOP
TM and TR
G/F, KS Lo Gallery, Hong Kong Park,
Admiralty
Tel: +852 2801 7177

☞ MOON GARDEN TEA HOUSE
TR
5 Hoi Ping Road
Tel: +852 2882 6878

Shanghai

☞ ANTIQUE TEA ROOM
Tea house
1315 Fuxing Xi Lu, Shanghai CN
Tel: +86 (0)21 6445 4625

☞ HUXINTING CHA GUAN
Tea house
Yu Yuan Garden, Pu Xi District,
Shanghai CN 200010
Tel: +86 (0)21 6373 6950

☞ JINGYUAN TEA HOUSE
AND ART GALLERY
1 Wu Lu Mu Qi Middle Road
Tel: +86 (0)21 6248 4132

☞ THE SOPHIA TEA HOUSE
480 Hua Shan Road, Pu Xi District,
Shanghai CN 200040
Tel: +86 (0)21 6249 9917; 6249 9723

☞ –YUAN YUAN YUAN
880 Heng Shan Road, Xu Jia Hui,
Shanghai CN, 200030
Tel: +86 (0)21 6438 8441; 6407 0441

TAIWAN

Taipei

☞ CHA FOR TEA
Tea house (Ten Ren Company)
No. 555 Chung Shan N. Road, sec 5,
Shihlin District, Taipei
Tel: +886 (0)2 888 2929

☞ LU YU TEA ART CENTER
(LUYU CHAYI ZHONGXIN)
Tea house with tasting classes
No. 64 Heng Yang Road, 2F, Taipei

☞ PING LIN TEA MUSEUM
Museum
No 19-1 Sung Chi Keng, Shui Te Tsun,
Ping Lin Village (center of Bao Zhong
production)
Tel: +886 (0)2 665 7251
Fax: +886 (0)2 665 6328

☞ WISTERIA TEA HOUSE (ZITENGLU)
Tea House
No. 1 Hsin Sheng South Road
Avenue 16, sec 3, Taipei
Tel: +886 (0)2 363 7375

JAPAN

In Japan there are two distinct kinds of tea: the
o cha, which is the traditional tea produced on
the archipelago, and the *ko cha*, which is the
foreign tea, generally red tea, either plain or
perfumed, and drunk as a Western luxury
product.

Western teas:
☞ LE PALAIS DES THÉS
several addresses in Tokyo (check the website:
www.palaisdesthes.com)

☞ MARIAGE FRÈRES:
several addresses in Tokyo and Kyoto
(check the website: www.mariagefreres.com)

Tokyo

Good Japanese tea can be found in all the
department stores, particularly the
Takashimaya chain.

Kyoto

Kyoto is the birthplace of traditional green tea
and Japanese tea ceremonies. It is in Kyoto that
the two major *cha no yu* schools are found: the
Urasenke and Omotesenke schools. Kyoto also
has numerous tea pavilions.

☞ HORAIDO
TM
www.kyoto-teramachi.or.jp/horaido
Teramachi Shijo Agaru – Nakagyo-ku
Tel: +81 (0)75 221 1215
Fax: +81 (0)75 213 2502

☞ IPPÔDÔ
TM and TR
www.ippodo-tea.co.jp
Teramachi Nijo Agaru – Nakagyo-ku
Tel: +81 (0)75 221 3421

☞ URASENKE FOUNDATION
Cha no yu *demonstrations*
Kamigoryômae Horikawa Agaru, Kamigyô-ku
Tel: +81 (0)75 431 6474

SINGAPORE

☞ LANGTRY'S
English style TR
www.theelizabeth.com
24 Mount Elizabeth, The Elizabeth,
Singapore 228518
Tel: +65 6738 1188 / Fax: +65 6732 3866
Station: Orchard

☞ TEA CHAPTER
Tea house
9A/11/11A Neil Road, Singapore 088808
Tel: +65 6226 1175; 6226 1917
Fax: +65 6221 0604
Station: Tanjong Pagar

SRI LANKA

As in other tea-producing countries, in Sri
Lanka most of the tea is exported; there is
therefore no real tea-drinking tradition and it
is difficult to find good tea to drink in the
country itself.

☞ TEA FACTORY
A former tea factory now converted into a
hotel, which produces its own tea. "Fresh" tea
is served in the mornings for early morning
tea.
www.aitkenspencehotels.com

AUSTRALIA

Sydney

☞ TEA TEMPLE
TM and TR
Level 2, Queen Victoria Building,
Sydney NSW 2000
Tel: +61 (0)2 9267 0582
Fax: +61 (0)2 9267 0583
Underground station: Town Hall

☞ THE TEA CENTER OF SYDNEY
TM and TR
146 Pitt Street Mall, Sydney NSW 2000
Tel: +61 (0)2 9223 9909
Fax: +61 (0)2 9221 7326
Underground station: Town Hall

Melbourne

☞ GRAY & SEDDON PREMIUM
TEA MERCHANTS
TM and TR
www.gray-seddon-tea.com
173 Centre Road, Bentleigh 3204
Tel: +61 3 9557 1906
Fax: +61 3 9557 8531

Bibliography

Bécaud Nadia, *Le Thé*, publ. Stéphane Bachès, 2004.

Blofeld John, *Thé et Tao, l'art chinois du thé*, Paris, publ. Albin Michel, collection "Espaces Libres,", 1997.

Bonheure Denis, *Le Théier*, Paris, publ. Maisonneuve et Larose, 1989.

Brochard Gilles, *À l'heure du thé*, Paris, publ. de l'Archipel, 2002.

Butel Paul, *Histoire du thé*, publ. Desjonquères, 1989.

Carles Michèle, Brochard Gilles, *Plaisirs de thé*, Paris, publ. du Chêne, 1998.

Chen Wei, *Le Thé, joyau de l'empire du Milieu*, publ. Quimétao, 2000.

De Morales Wenceslau, *Le Culte du thé*, Paris, publ. La Différence, 1998.

Finkoff Michel, Bernard Philippe (photos), *Mes jardins de thé: voyage dans les plantations de Ceylan à Darjeeling*, Paris, publ. Albin Michel, 1990.

Fortune Robert, *La Route du thé et des fleurs*, Paris, publ. Payot, 1994.

Gong Gang et Paul Ariès, *Le Goût*, publ. Desclée de Brouwer and Presses littéraires et artistiques de Shanghai, 2000.

Hal Fatema, *Les Saveurs et les Gestes*, Paris, publ. Stock, 1996.

Inoué Yasushi, *Le Maître de thé*, Paris, publ. Stock, 1998.

Johnson Dorothea, James Norwood Pratt (intro), *Tea & Etiquette: Taking Tea for Business and Pleasure*, Sterling, VA, publ. Capital Books, 2000.

Jumeau-Laffond Jacques, Yi Sabine, *Le Livre de l'amateur de thé*, Paris, publ. Robert Laffont, 1990.

Langley Andrew, *The Little Book of Tea Tips*, London, publ. Absolute Press, 2005.

Lao She, *La Maison de thé*, publ. Langues étrangères, 1980.

Lu Yu, *Le Classique du thé*, traduit par Sister Jean-Marie Vianney, publ. Morel, 1977.

Lu Yu, *Le Cha Jing ou Classique du Thé*, traduit par Véronique Chevaleyre, publ. Jean-Claude Gawsewitch, 2004.

Mariage Frères, *Éloge de la cuisine au thé*, Paris, publ. Hachette, 2002.

Mitscher Lester, Victoria Dolby, *The Green Tea Book: China's Fountain of Youth*, New York, publ. Avery Publishing, 1997.

Monod Théodore, *Méharées: Explorations au vrai Sahara*, Arles, publ. Actes Sud, collection "Terres d'aventure," 1994.

Montseren Jean, *Guide de l'amateur de thé*, Paris, publ. Solar, 1999.

Okakura Kakuzô, *The Book of Tea*, Arles, publ. Philippe Picquier, 1996.

Pascualini D.T., Suet Bruno (photos), *Le Temps du thé*, Paris, publ. Marval, 1999.

Perrier-Robert Annie, *Book of Tea*, London, publ. Hachette Illustrated UK, 2004.

Perry Sara and Alison Miksch, *The New Tea Book: A Guide to Black, Green, Herbal and Chai Teas*, San Francisco, publ. Chronicle Books, 2001.

Pettigrew Jane, *The Tea Companion*, (Connoisseur Guides), Running Press Book Publishers, 2004.

Praudel Andoche, *Essai sur la céramique japonaise depuis les origines*, publ. You-Feng, 2001.

Richardson Bruce, *The Great Tea Rooms of America*, Kentucky, publ. Benjamin Press, 2006.

Richardson Shelley, Bruce Richardson, *Tea for All Seasons*, Beaver Dam, publ. Partners Publishing Group, 2002.

Romain Hyppolite (textes et dessins), Romain Yann (photos), *Le Thé en Chine*, Geneva, publ. Minerva, 2002.

Sangmanee Kitty Cha, *La Route du thé, le triangle d'or*, Paris, publ. Hazan, 2001.

Sen Hounsai Genshitsu, *The Book of Tea: The Classic Work on the Japanese Tea Ceremony and the Value of Beauty*, Tokyo, publ. Kodansha, 2006.

Sen Soshitsu, *Vie du thé, esprit du thé*, publ. Jean Cyrille Godefroy, 1994.

Shimizu Christine, editor-in-chief, *Les Arts de la cérémonie du thé*, Dijon, publ. Faton, 1996.

Simpson Helen, *The London Ritz Book of Afternoon Tea: The Art and Pleasures of Taking Tea*, London, publ. Ebury Press, 2006.

Smith Michael, Michael R.P. Bartlett, *The Afternoon Tea Book*, New Jersey, publ. John Wiley & Sons, 1989.

Sôseki Natsume, *Oreiller d'herbes*, Paris, publ. Rivages, 1987.

Soutel-Gouiffes Juliette, *La Voie des quatre vertus*, publ. La Table d'Émeraude, 1995.

This Hervé, *Les Secrets de la casserole*, Paris, publ. Belin.

Ukers William Harrison, *All About Tea*, 1935.

Valfré Patrice, *Yixing: des théières pour l'Europe*, publ. Exotic Line, 2000.

Walter Marc, *The Book of Tea*, Paris, publ. Flammarion, 1991.

Zak Victoria, *Twenty Thousand Secrets of Tea: The Most Effective Ways to Benefit from Nature's Healing Herbs*, New York, publ. Dell, 1999.

(collective work) *L'Extase du thé*, translated from the Chinese by Wing-fun Cheng and Hervé Collet, publ. Moundarren, 2002.

(collective work) *Tea for 2, les rituels du thé dans le monde*, Belgium, publ. Crédit Communal, 1999.

Acknowledgments

THE AUTHOR WOULD LIKE TO THANK:
FOR THEIR KNOWLEDGE OF, AND OPENNESS TO, THE WORLD
OF TEA
Mathilde Laurent
Anne-Marie Rosenberg
Chloë Doutre-Roussel
Jacques Genin
Pierre Massia

FOR THEIR ENLIGHTENED ADVICE
Vivien Messavant
Alain Laurens
Yasumori Nagahiro
Nathalie Boireau
Évelyne Lejeune-Resnick

FOR THEIR WARM WELCOME
Chai 33
Chajin
Mademoiselle Li
Kusmi Tea
Le Comptoir Long Jing
Pâtisserie Tesnime
Simple Simon Salon de Thé
Thés de Chine

FOR THE FRUITS OF SEVERAL YEARS' COLLABORATION
François-Xavier Delmas of the Palais des Thés
Philippe Martin of Studio Mallet & Martin
Olivier Kaba, Mathilde Laurent, and Carine Baudry

And everyone in the Aubanel team, in particular
Anne Serroy, Sabine Kuentz, and Sophie Gallet.

Photographic credits

All the photographs in this book are by JEAN-FRANÇOIS MALLET
with the exception of photos on the following pages:

☞ cover page (small inset), p. 6 (top), p. 8, p. 12 (all three), p. 15, p. 18, p. 22,
p. 25, p. 37 (two on the left), p. 48, p. 51 (bottom), p. 52, p. 55 (left), p. 54,
p. 58, p. 63 (top), p. 77, p. 85 (right), p. 100 (top and middle), p. 154, p. 159
(middle and bottom), p. 165 (left), and p. 170 (right): by CORBIS

☞ p. 7, p. 51 (top), pp. 56–57, p. 61 (two top photos), p. 64, p. 65, p. 75 (left),
p. 76, p. 78 (right), p. 79, pp. 82–83, p. 84, p. 159 (top), p. 167 (top), and
p. 170 (left): by LYDIA GAUTIER

☞ p. 9, p. 29, p. 51 (middle), p. 53, pp. 64–65, p. 72, p. 80, p. 85 (left), and
p. 175: by HOA-QUI

☞ p. 75 (right), p. 107 (left), p. 109, p. 134, p. 149 (two on the left), and p. 175:
by BRUNO SUET

☞ p. 26, p. 33 (right), p. 78 (left), p. 94, and p. 122 (right): by ÉRIC MORIN